1978

Child Abuser

Child Abuser
A Study of Child Abusers in Self-help Group Therapy

Marilyn C. Collins, Ph.D.

PSG Publishing Company, Inc.
Littleton, Massachusetts

Library of Congress Cataloging in Publication Data

Collins, Marilyn C.   1947-
    Child abuser.

    Vita.
    Bibliography: p.
    1. Child abuse.   2. Self-help groups—United
States.   I. Title.   [DNLM: 1. Child abuse.
2. Parents.   Psychotherapy, Group.   WA320 C7140]
HV6741.C543   362.7'1   76-47866
ISBN 0-88416-186-2

Printed in the United States of America.

International Standard Book Number: 0-88416-186-2

Library of Congress Catalog Card Number: 76-47866

To Steve, who saw the butterfly before I did

CHILDREN'S BLUES

So many times...in the middle of the night
  Your mama and your daddy...in a great big
  fight.
Slammin' and a screamin'...callin' out names.
  To their little children bring a whole lot of pain.

    And that's how, yeah that's how, that's how
    Some children learn to sing the blues.

And at the dinner table...in the middle of the bite
  There's nobody talkin'...'ya know it just ain't
  right.
And it's so hard to swallow...it sticks in your
throat...
  'Ya wanna run away child...but ain't no place to
  go.

    And that's how, yeah that's how, that's how
    Some children learn to sing the blues.

Then they send you off to school...in ole' hand me
down clothes
  'Ya got holes in your soles...'ya think this
  whole world knows.
And some of the people treat 'ya...just like you're
not quite as good...
  It gets harder and harder just to do as good as
  you should.

    And that's how, yeah that's how, that's how
    Some
      children
        learn
          to
            sing
              the
                blues...

            —Bonnie Koloc

CONTENTS

ACKNOWLEDGEMENTS

This book would never have reached completion were it not for the assistance and the encouragement of various individuals. I want first to acknowledge, with appreciation and affection, Howard S. Becker, who "learned me the river" at a time when I thought I would surely drown in it and who was supportive from the very beginning of this project. I am grateful to Bernard Beck for his guidance and candor in convincing me that I was worthy of the project, and for his understanding of the worthlessness of the word "custody." I am also grateful to Marijean Suelzle, who was always willing to share her time and expertise and who endured my sporadic incoherencies without complaint. Receiving the counsel of these individuals was a professional privilege.

In many ways, the consummation of this research project has been a family affair. I must express my gratitude to my sainted *veve* Maria and to *yiayia* Stella who lovingly babysat and babysat and babysat so that I could carry on with my work. I wish to thank my dear sweet Aunt Helen who typed draft after draft of the manuscript for me. To my son Billy, who is too young to realize the amount of my time and attention he has been denied, a mere thank you is insufficient. I wish also to thank my parents who, years and years ago, in the days of the Star Cafe, Durham, and Franklinton, instilled within me the desire to achieve an "impossible dream."

To the members of Parents Anonymous who participated in the study and whom I regard affectionately as "my child abusers," I am particularly indebted, for it was they who taught me that Oz never really gave the Tin Man what he didn't already have.

I wish to thank Northwestern University and the National Institute of Mental Health for the financial assistance I received in the way of a scholarship (1972-1973) and a fellowship (1973-1976) which made possible my pursuit of a graduate education.

Finally I wish to thank the Honorable Judge Arthur N. Hamilton, Circuit Court Judge, Juvenile Court of Cook County, Illinois, for his gracious generosity in permitting me to use his courtroom as a laboratory to conduct much of my initial research.

Marilyn C. Collins, Ph.D.

1 INTRODUCTION

It was a little after 7:30 P.M. on a weekday evening early in October when eight women entered a room in a Chicago Park District Building. They had been meeting regularly in that room on a weekly basis for about a year. They usually sat in folding chairs around a conference table in a room used for storing filing cabinets, coatracks, brooms, old furniture, and stacks of ash trays.

There was nothing that an observer might describe as singular about the appearance of these women. Most were modestly attired in slacks and blouses or skirts and sweaters. Some were a little overweight; other seemed underweight. Some, whose means of transportation was the Chicago Transit Authority, had stopped to do some shopping before coming to the meeting and were carrying shopping bags. Outwardly there were no indicators that might be of some assistance to an observer trying to predict the kind of activity in which these women were participants in that room in the Park District Building. Some women brought coffee to drink, others brought soda pop; some crocheted or chain-smoked. As I entered the room, their meeting had already begun and some of the women were talking:

Toby: In my case I build a wall up and when I try to go on the road of being a nice person, that wall is taken down...inch by inch, and I build up that wall. To me it is security. If you don't let nothing in, nothing can hurt you. But I don't wanna be like that...

Francine: Well, at least I'm trying; my husband is really a pretty good type but I don't know how long he's gonna hold out. Because I'm not holding out, so...like, um, when I was trying, for so many years I've been trying to put the picture together. A lot of it is still pieces of the puzzle...

Mary: How old were you then?

1

Francine: Six, seven. I was taken away—I didn't go back home until I was fourteen. And they were separated already then. And, um, like things...I remember some things about it, some of the things that my mother did to me. Finally I sat my dad down and I said, you tell me what happened, before I go out of my mind.

Mary: In other words, why were you so abused.

Francine: Oh, I knew pieces, because I knew...

Mary: You wanted the whole thing?

Francine: Yeah...I remember some of the beatings and fights, and the social workers, somebody came in, stripping me down, looking at the bruises. You know, just glimpses that were like a dream. So I told him, you tell me what happened because it was driving me nuts, you know?

Mary: Did he?

Francine: Yeah, he told me.

Mary: Do you understand?

Francine: Some of it, yeah...but not really. I mean, I don't understand why, you know, my mother did these things. Like I'm really gonna try to understand it.

Mary: Possibly you won't do those same things?

Francine: I have to work with children and with mothers, and I find myself saying the wrong things to, to, like, to mothers with little babies...

Mary: Like what?

Francine: You know, like the reason, like I see these kids and it brings me an awful picture of life. It makes me feel...I see myself at that age and I work in pediatrics. And in the maternity area where I see the mothers with the kids. I just all of a sudden get a fear, I don't know, or maybe I sympathize. Maybe I feel sorry for myself. Or wonder, are they ever gonna have that, you know, or something.

Toby: Do you ever think that what you're feeling, ah, could be mixed up with resentment for the fact that these kids are with their mothers and you recall your childhood?

Francine: I've thought about that, too, yeah. You know, it's a whole bunch of things. I'm just trying to single it out, and there's the whole thing about my husband, and maybe I've had so many fears about it...but it was the pediatrics books that really kill me. Well, the child-abuse syndrome and the character defects, and most of the time it was due to the fact that the parents did that to you at home. That's just what I didn't want to read. [laughing] Here I am, being...I was taken away and all these things...

Sylvia: So when you read those books, is there ever a section that says this cycle can be changed?

Francine: No, that's just it...and it's really sad, because I know that, okay, the alcoholic can be changed...so can other people, you know, and I realize this all the time and yet, well, up until now, I haven't really made an effort, you know, to go out and get help. When I think it was, um, I was in the hospital myself and the...see, I was adopted, and then I was taken away. That's like adding insult to injury. You're running, you know, you find out you're adopted, you're already feeling rejection. I don't know why. I remember that, that it made me feel like somebody didn't want you. Then...and [laugh] and then you're taken away again, that's another rejection... that's two. And it keeps adding up to the point where you want people to reject you. Even your husband.

Toby: Maybe, because people take that as a personal failure. Instead of looking at it as a failure that someone else has. And has nothing to do with you. It's their inability to cope within their environment, and whether it was you or anybody else, it wouldn't make any difference.

Francine: I know, but at the time...

Margie: But placing the burden on yourself, you always go around saying what is wrong with me. Then people can't respond to you positively. And the particular people that you end up hooking yourself with can't respond positively to themselves.

(Field notes, October 24, 1974)

The group of parents we followed into that room in the Park District Building were similar to many other parents across the United States who meet in regular weekly groups to share and get help for problems they have in child rearing. They are members of an organization called Parents Anonymous, a crisis intervention program set up to help prevent damaging relationships between parents and their children. The organization was founded in 1970 by Jolly K., the pseudonym of a young California woman who was frustrated and angered by the lack of treatment resources in her state available to parents with a child-abuse problem.

PURPOSES AND THEMES

In this study we will look at the lives of individuals who become affiliated with this organization which is based on self-help group therapy. We will be looking at how parents:

1. Mature in this self-help group therapy program which acts as a socializing agent in their lives

2. Find and create roles for themselves as lay professionals in the field of child abuse

3. Construct a life "career" from their affiliation with Parents Anonymous which is based on the acceptance of the label of child abuser

4. Deal with the process of transforming this discrediting label or information into positive data

The third point is of paramount importance for our study, and in a later discussion we will argue that the process by which discrediting information is transformed into positive data occurs subsequent to the act of joining Parents Anonymous and prior to committing oneself to the organization and making a "career" of the affiliation.

Before proceeding further, a brief discussion of how a person may come to affiliate with Parents Anonymous is relevant.

AFFILIATION

Some of the parents who affiliate with Parents Anonymous may do so voluntarily. There is a variety of ways that the organization's existence comes to be known to those who are in need of its services. For example, parents may read about the organization in a community newspaper or hear about it on the radio or on television. If they feel they need the services the organization offers, they may voluntarily seek out those services. Or parents may have occasion to use the facilities of an emergency room in a hospital for physical injuries that they have inflicted on their child; a staff person may mention the existence of the organization in a suggestive manner while providing the parent with some of the organization's literature.

Not all the parents join Parents Anonymous voluntarily; some are forced to join and to attend meetings regularly. Again, the methods of involuntary membership may be as varied and circuitous as the methods of voluntary membership. We hope the following examples will describe more clearly the process that involuntary affiliation might involve.

For instance, a working parent may place one or more children in a day-care center while he or she is at work. A day-care center worker may notice cuts or bruises on one of the children and suspect that the bruises were not accidentally inflicted—in other words, the injuries appear to have been inflicted by another person. Then the day-care center worker may ask the child how he or she got those bruises or marks, and the child may respond, "My mommy did it." The worker may then question the parent about the marks; the parent's explanation may not coincide with the child's explanation, or the explanation may be incongruent with the severity or nature of the injuries. If at this point there is any incongruity between the parent's history of the injury and the nature and severity of the physical trauma, the suspicion of abuse develops.

Illinois law mandates a wide range of people to report suspected cases of child abuse to the Illinois Department of Children and Family Services and to the police. Once the report has been filed, a social worker is assigned to the case representing the Illinois Department of Children and Family Services, the day-care center, or other agencies. The social worker investigates the case, which may involve visiting the child's home and interviewing the parents and the child as well as making a general assessment of the adequacy of the environment in which the child lives. If the social worker's report is of a negative nature, then in all likelihood the entire situation will come to the attention of the judge hearing abuse and neglect cases in that jurisdiction.

Once the case is in court, the state will request that the child allegedly being abused in the natural environment be placed in a foster environment for a time. After a decision is reached, the judge may turn to the parents suspected of perpetrating the abuse and strongly recommend that they seek outside counseling for themselves. The strong recommendation is usually in the form of a court order, which also may stipulate that the parents seek out and start attending Parents Anonymous sessions regularly for additional therapy and support. It is also then stipulated that the social worker who filed the report make periodic checks to find out if the parents are indeed obeying the court order.

Question: How did you first hear about Parents Anonymous?

Response: Probably through the case worker working in foster care. She had mentioned it one time as an alternative thing. I never thought much of it. I didn't pursue it any further. (Interview #5)

Response: I heard about it on a radio program. It just seemed to apply to me and about anger and yelling at your kids and letting your anger out on them when you were mad at something else. (Interview #1)

Response: I must have seen something on television...a couple of years ago. I wasn't too much aware of it until my counselor wrote me a letter over the summer. She didn't say much...this is an organization where they help each other and it would be beneficial to me as far as meeting new friends and working out problems...she thought this would be an improvement. (Interview #2)

Response: I saw you on television and I saw the telephone number flashed across the screen. (Interview #7)

Response: It was a television program on one evening. I was sitting at the dinner table screaming at everybody...practically choking on my food, and the program came on and I saw there was a number given and a sponsor's name. I immediately jotted it down and the next day I called the television station. It was like the last straw. I was absolutely as miserable as I could possibly be. I called and started coming to the meetings. (Interview #9)

Response: Through a girl who was living in the building I was living in. She was going to Parents Anonymous. She bugged me to go. I was scared of it because I didn't know what it was all about. She was a woman who had her children taken away from her. I just didn't know what to think. (Interview #8)

Response: The first time that I heard about it was through a *Woman's Day* magazine article. I had been reading it at my doctor's office. My God! This sounds fantastic!

Question: You thought it was fantastic. What about it was fantastic?

Response: I realized that I could not possibly be the only parent that felt so unsure. Almost as though a chair was pulled out from underneath them. Not knowing what to do. Not knowing what to do in many situations. I knew I couldn't be the only one with the frustrations and anxieties. Parents don't talk about it. Women don't talk about it. They feel that it's a reflection that they are bad parents. That they shouldn't have these feelings about their child or children. I thought it was a marvelous idea that there would be a group that parents could go to, to seek help for themselves. To relieve themselves of the burdens that they were carrying around inside that they couldn't talk about to anybody else because nobody would accept it. (Interview #11)

Question: What was the nature of the information you received about Parents Anonymous?

Response: My first opinion was that it was a bunch of people that...I don't know. When I thought of abusing a child, I thought of broken arms and broken legs. Violent people. And the thought of going in and being with people like this turned me off. I did a lot of cruel things, but I never broke an arm or a leg. This was the impression that I had been given.

Question: Did you think Parents Anonymous was for people who did those kinds of things?

Response: Yes.

Question: What did you think of Parents Anonymous when you talked to the person on the hotline?

Response: I didn't want any part of it at all.

Question: What did you think the other members would be like?

Response: I thought they would be very violent people...the type of people I wouldn't want to associate with.

Question: What did you think happened at the meetings? Did the hotline give you any idea?

Response: No...I don't think they even knew.

Question: How is it that you finally did get to go to a first meeting?

Response One Saturday afternoon I was watching the television, and all of a sudden I saw a girlfriend of mine. It was

Sherry. Sherry was in my group therapy. She and I had gotten to know each other real well. All of a sudden I see her on television talking about Parents Anonymous and her feelings about her children, the way she was brought up. I watched her. After the program was over, I got on the phone and said, "Sherry, I didn't know you beat your kids, why didn't you tell me?" And she said, "Jane, I wanted to, but I didn't know how to tell you." Had I not seen a friend who could not talk to me about her problem, couldn't confront me with the fact that she knew I had a problem? She understood. Like I said, in this therapy we were in, we're not allowed to talk about our children. She was the one who introduced me to it [Parents Anonymous] and told me about the meetings and asked if I would like to go. I said yes, I would. I found it completely different from what I had expected. I found they were very friendly people who looked like normal, happy, everyday people. They made me feel very warm and welcome...it was like I was immediately their friend. (Interview #13)

Response: There was this incident where my two-year-old son ran away from home and I had the police come down real heavy on me. After this incident they [police] decided they would finally kick in and give me a hand, figuring I would never get the children back. They gave me a list of six different places to call. I just thought I would start with one, Parents Anonymous, and if that didn't help me I would go to another. So far, Parents Anonymous has helped me. I can't complain. (Interview #17)

The purpose of the previous quotations and illustrations was, first, to assist the reader in differentiating among the various methods of affiliation utilized by parents in search of help for a child-abuse problem and, second, to destroy the myth that these self-help therapy groups include only persons who *want* help for a problem they themselves recognize. Nearly one-third of the individuals in our sample were mandated by persons in positions of authority, such as a school social worker or a judge, to attend Parents Anonymous sessions to avoid forfeiting parental custody rights. These non-self-referred parents approach the organization with hostility and distrust, and unlike the self-referred group, have difficulty in relating to the label of child abuser. However, once they make the initial affiliation step of becoming involved as a participant in weekly group sessions, there is an insignificant difference between the way they and the self-referred parents respond to the stimulus of Parents Anonymous as an adult socializing agent.

Voluntary Affiliation

Question: If you were to compare or contrast other groups or another group that you've been a member of to Parents Anonymous, what would you say is unique or different about being a member of Parents Anonymous?

Response: The difference is that you can say whatever you want about how you feel towards yourself and towards the children without anyone labeling you as "bad." The follow-up that goes on everyday all day—the fact that you've had constant support, you have somebody else you can turn to when you feel that something is going to go bad. Or sometimes when you get the feeling that something very good has happened and you're so happy that you share it with someone else. Many times that can bring them out of different states of depression, too. I don't have much of a family feeling with my family, no peers my own age and really no support from parents or anybody. Really, the group gave me, I guess, what family would have if I had had somebody to talk to. (Interview #4)

Involuntary Affiliation

Question: If you were to compare other groups to being a member of P.A., what is unique about being a member of P.A. as opposed to your counseling experience elsewhere?

Response: The sponsor won't probe into, uh...when you relate an incident, she won't say...why did you do it?...what were you feeling at the time? or, how do you feel?...a standard phrase you hear all the time. And this is something she doesn't do. Right away she looks for alternatives to the situation. She won't ask me, how do you feel after you hit him? This is something the group does. That's a big difference there. I think it's an important one.

Question: Could you be specific and tell me how it is that you think that P.A. helps?

Response: Well, when you go in there it isn't...the girls know that I have an abuse problem, so they can talk to me, and it isn't like you're talking to someone, you know, who says, what makes you do that? They don't come back with, how can you possibly hit your child like that? It's someone who has the same problem, even if it isn't as bad. Maybe it's someone who has a worse problem, but someone you can talk to and understand, someone is always there you can call, whether it's 2 o'clock in the morning or 2 o'clock in the afternoon...

there's someone if you called who would talk to you. (Interview #28)

Voluntary Affiliation

Question: What would you say is unique or different about Parents Anonymous?

Response: I don't know. I think it's a group that works on a person feeling better about themself. I haven't been involved in that many groups to know. They handle it very well. To come out of their shell and make them better basically by the problems that are brought out. For example, talking about or like...''I did *this* today.'' Then you go back and ask...how did it start?...what were your feelings when it started?...what started happening when you started feeling this way?...was anything happening outside, or had something happened the day before?...had you received a call from a parent, husband, or boyfriend to kind of set you off? Things that you don't consciously realize are doing it to you and helping abuse come out in you. Maybe you can't go somewhere you were counting on going to, or maybe you've had a change of plans. I know that sounds so minor, but the kids come in and they start bothering you and you are upset anyway. It keeps building and building. I think the P.A. group goes back and tries to find out what happened during the day. What happened to start it. They deal with things like that, *but* only if you want to. Only if you *want* to tell someone what happened. (Interview #9)

Involuntary Affiliation

Question: Have you ever been affiliated with any other group before you joined P.A.?

Response: No. My therapist wanted me to join [a] group and I backed out of it.

Question: Was that private counseling you were involved in?

Response: Yes, but she told me that I'd better go join a group. I couldn't handle it. At first I said yes, and then I called them up and said I couldn't do it. I was scared just to talk to them.

Question: Have any problems been created for you as a Parents Anonymous member? Any problems between you and your family?

Response: No, but I don't really get along with them...I don't know if it's me...my mother says she sees a change but I don't see it.

She says I seem much calmer, I seem so much better able to get closer to my family. Christmas Eve was the biggest gift, I got closer to my family. I know the group is just great for me. It helped me to even get along with Fran who's got more money than anyone in our family and who I always resented...I actually got along with her on Christmas Eve! I really dreaded family things before, but the group has really helped me...they say I'm changing, but I know it's because of my P.A. group. They bring in certain things [suggestions] in the group and it really works. I don't mean they say that this is the way you *have* to do something. Certain things come out of the group sessions, and you go home and all of a sudden...I would have never gotten through Christmas Eve if it wasn't for the group. I'm being honest with you, I get real nervous when people come over.

Question: Do you think that since you've been a member of Parents Anonymous that it has changed you in any way? You mentioned earlier that you stop and think before you do certain things. Has it changed you that way?

Response: I think it's made me more aware. I think the only way that you can change yourself is to become aware of yourself. The group has helped me to become aware of a lot of things about myself. Like I used to always get on my kid's back for his report cards and his marks in school, and now I just leave him alone. That's a big step because I've been a perfectionist all my life with grades and education. I don't like errors or erased papers because it looks like you've just let everything go. I don't like that. My kid used to really catch it from me. Yeah, it made me become more aware of me. (Interview #32)

This insignificant difference in response between self-referred and institutionally referred parents is important for the following reasons:

1. There is a paucity of research in the area of self-help movements and their demonstrable effects on adult socialization in adult life crisis

2. Most self-help movements place virtually no trust and faith in the "professional" and operate successfully and effectively while being free of professional dominance

3. The success of countless self-help programs, such as Alcoholics Anonymous, Weight Watchers, Gamanon, poses the question of how the myth of self-help as an impotent therapeutic "modality" has managed to survive;

unless, of course, the promulgators of the myth are professionals of dubious integrity who are threatened by programs based on the theory that the person in need is quite capable of defining and labeling those needs

SCOPE OF THIS BOOK

Our investigation does not directly address such difficult questions as whether professionals threatened by self-help therapy and seeing it as an infringement on their domain retaliate by describing group self-help therapy as impotent and ineffectual. The materials presented, however, will bear relevance to such questions.

Also, we will not directly address and answer questions of cause and control of child abuse; at best, such discussions are inelegantly subjective and lack empirical support. But here, too, the materials presented will bear relevance to the cause, prevention, and control of child abuse.

For the usefulness of other interests and to provide the reader with at least a modicum of material enabling him or her to assess the arguments made, we will include many direct quotations from interviews of parents who are members of Parents Anonymous, such as those presented in the first few pages of this chapter.

As previously mentioned, our investigation will consider how parents mature, or come of age, in self-help therapy groups; also, we will present and develop the argument that the self-help therapy group experiences act as an agent of socialization in the lives of the people involved. We will also be concerned with how participants in the self-help therapy group find and create roles or occupational categories for themselves as "lay professionals" in the field of child abuse, where the "professional" dominates. And last, but by no means least, we will rely heavily on Goffman's concept of moral career—i.e., "the regular sequence of changes...in the person's self and his framework of imagery for judging himself and others which he shares with others by virtue of common membership in a social category" (1961: 128)—and will focus our attention on the "moral career" of a child abuser.

The moral career of a child abuser implies neither success nor failure, but rather a natural transformation or natural evolution with respect to self-image, skill development, and social functioning. The concept of moral career is useful in explaining the relationship between response and self-image over time, and it is our belief that this concept can be grounded and illustrated in our study. We will see the way people, juxtaposing the puzzle pieces of their lives, construct "careers" based on self-acceptance and the completion of a process involving the transformation of discrediting information or a discrediting label into positive data.

The central theme of this study will be that, unlike the careers of most persons defined as deviant and processed through specialized institutions, the careers of child abusers who are helped run a course toward self-acceptance and moral reinstatement. The way in which this moral reinstatement transpires—particularly, the way the settings studied rally in support of such reinstatement—and the consequential events surrounding such reinstatement are the central thematic threads of this study.

Because this researcher participated extensively in the everyday lives and experiences of people involved in group self-help therapy, it is possible to see how the parents themselves view their circumstances and the role that group self-help therapy plays in their lives. While we are not interested in generalizing to all persons involved in self-help therapy, it is our hope that our detailed account will serve as a springboard for more widely based research of self-help therapy groups as agents of socialization for adults in life crisis situations. We intend to demonstrate that these parents involved in Parents Anonymous change the deteriorating parent-child relationship defined and labeled "child abuse" by finding a "place in the sun" for themselves within the framework of the group. We will argue that this framework offers them a chance to move *away* from their negative self-image *toward* self-acceptance and moral reinstatement, which in turn enables them to function socially in a variety of areas as adults, and particularly as parents. Furthermore, we would proffer that if it is indeed the process of transforming discrediting information about oneself into positive information that is experienced as a "career affiliate" of Parents Anonymous, and if this experience of positive self-image development serves to retard abusive tendencies, then the most successful preventive program that any agency or institution at the local, state, or federal levels could offer would be one which would:

1. Facilitate the emergence of these self-help therapy groups

2. Facilitate the emancipation of these self-help therapy groups from the agency or institution which assisted in their emergence

3. Allow the self-help therapy groups to take on organizational lives of their own

This first chapter has been devoted to stating the purposes, intentions, major themes, and central issues of our study. In the following chapter we discuss the role of this author, both as researcher and participant, in the research project and address the question of the sociologist as participant, as expert, and as objective observer. Included in the description of the research setting are the methods utilized in the gathering of the data for the project as well as the method employed in the analysis of the data.

In Chapter 3 we focus our attention on the impetus for the project and the basic research questions. Preliminary to our discussion of the basic research questions, we describe in detail the organization called Parents Anonymous by examining its stated purposes and the population it seeks to serve. In addition, we analyze the basis of the organizational model as well as its rationale.

In Chapter 4 we look at the moral career of a child abuser by analyzing the processes involved in accepting the label of child abuser and in becoming an ex-child abuser. Based on extensive observation we present and describe the six stages that a child abuser who is a member of Parents Anonymous goes through before discrediting information is transformed into positive data.

In our final chapter we continue to address the question of how participation in, and affiliation with, these self-help therapy groups are useful in adult socialization; to do this, we show that these self-help therapy groups serve as catalysts in raising the individual's awareness of emerging self-motivation. Further, we posit that this awareness of motivational emergence comes from a sequence of social experiences involving affiliation and that this affiliation develops naturally into what we define and describe as a "career of affiliation." In our conclusion we also comment generally about the failure of rehabilitative programs dealing with child abusers by pointing primarily to their inability to help provide for the child abuser a sequence of social experiences which would serve as catalysts in raising the child abuser's awareness of his or her emerging self-motivation.

Throughout the study we make extensive use of what the people involved in self-help therapy groups make of their experiences and how they deal with them.

2 METHODS

Go and sit in the lounges of the luxury hotels and on the doorsteps of the flop-houses; sit on the Gold Coast settees and on the slum shakedowns; sit in the Orchestra Hall and in the Star and Garter Burlesk. In short...go get the seats of your pants dirty in real research....
(Robert E. Park: cited in McKinney, 1966: 71)

In this study we observed individuals involved in self-help therapy groups designed to help child abusers change their abusive behaviors. Much has been written in the way of etiological explanations with respect to child abuse (see Bibliography for specific references to articles and books dealing with this topic). Both medicine and law have contributed descriptions and definitions adequately depicting the activity of child abuse as well as the individual child abusers. Very little, however, has been written about how these individuals *see themselves* and their role in the activity. Due to the dearth of data in this area, medicine and law have been unable to provide us with more of an understanding of the needs, problems, and desires of these people, or of the seemingly mundane occurrences that affect the lives of these individuals daily.

For example, if we look at the present definitions of child abuse or at the battered-child syndrome as defined by C. Henry Kempe (1961) and later supported by David G. Gil's research efforts of the late 1960s and early 1970s, we find the activity basically described as a nonaccidental physical attack intentionally inflicted on a child by a caretaker. This tells us no more than is visible to any eye, trained or untrained. Nowhere in the literature do we find the question of the activity's definition and description put to the participant or practitioner of the activity; yet proposed quasi-solutions to the problem of child abuse are abundant. These proposals come from onlookers who appear to be ignoring and avoiding the practitioner's description of

15

what goes on. This may be attributed to the fact that heretofore the field of child abuse—whether research, treatment, or social policy—has been dominated by physicians, psychiatrists, and law enforcers, chiefly because it is felt that they are able to see things other people cannot. They *do* see things others would fail to recognize because they have been *trained* to see these things, just as social scientists have been trained to see things that others would fail to recognize. However, "sociological vision" is as integral a part of looking at society and its maladies as are medical, psychiatric, or legal visions. As we began our research we found a gap between how the dominant professions articulated the problem of child abuse and how the practitioners themselves viewed the problem and their relationship to it.

In this study we have tried to expose this prodigious lacuna in method in the hope that it might serve as a warning to those who would define the actions of others while allowing only a modicum of input *from those others.* We strongly believe that unless an overt attempt is made to establish some congruence between the onlooker's definition of child abuse and the practitioner's definition of the activity and its meaning, there will be little, if any, change with respect to the practitioner's behavior and self-definition. In attempting to establish this congruence we spent long periods during the course of our research gathering data by observing the practitioner in a variety of contexts, i.e., at home, work, court, play, and Parents Anonymous meetings.

The study began in the fall of 1972 while I was conducting a fieldwork study of the proceedings and daily routines endemic to Calendar Seven of the Juvenile Court of Cook County, Illinois. I spent over six months observing, informally interviewing, and just plain hanging around the courtroom "players"—public defenders, assistant state's attorneys, court reporters, sheriffs, judges, probation officers, social workers, and alleged child abusers. Sometimes I sat in the jurybox of the courtroom and recorded my fieldnotes and observed. Occasionally I would sit in the waiting area with the alleged child abusers, recording my fieldnotes while observing their behavior. It took me nowhere. The data I was amassing had everything to do with courtroom procedure and the ins and outs of bureaucratic dealings, but it had little bearing on how people came to be suspected child abusers, what their daily lives were like, how they felt about themselves and their actions, how they defined their needs, and basically how they were different from, or similar to, any other person you might meet during the course of the day.

I modified my tactics. I stopped spending so much time in the courtroom and concentrated my efforts in the waiting area where the alleged child abusers awaited their turn to approach the judge. During their waiting period, which usually lasted for hours, I tried talking to them casually about miscellaneous topics: why they were there, the weather, did they know anything about the judge, were they satisfied with their legal representation, did they have a social worker and what did they think of him or her, and endlessly on. Again, this approach was taking me nowhere and even caused problems. First, the judge expressed his disappointment in my changed tactics and appeared offended because it seemed as though I no longer regarded him or his courtroom worthy of research. Then the assistant state's attorneys and public defenders, in an effort to entice me back into the courtroom, made promises about opening up their confidential files to me and sharing some of the psychiatric evaluations of "those people waiting to see the judge." These files, and write-ups, all stamped CONFIDENTIAL, were literally given to me—some of them are still in my possession—as a bribe to come back into the courtroom rather than study the people in the waiting room. (One might begin to ponder to what lengths people will go in their efforts to control and manipulate if a lowly social researcher is offered access to confidential material which she never requested.) The larger issue, however, is that they felt I would be going about my research blindly unless I let them explain and interpret everything *for* me. For instance, many times while I was sitting alone in the jurybox observing, the assistant state's attorney, while he was presenting evidence to the judge, would approach me and say, "Are you taking this down? You should be."

As I continued my vigil out in the waiting area casually interviewing the waiting people, I lost more and more rapport with the courtroom "players." The court reporters and probation officers stopped talking to me, and the sheriff's police requested to see my visitor's pass with increased frequency. Then, as if it had been orchestrated, the alleged child abusers in the waiting room recoiled from me. They would talk to me ever so briefly only about such things as the weather or how hideous the waiting was. The ones who thought about talking to me attempted what we might call a "research bargain": they would tell me their story if I would put in a good word for them with the judge. When I explained I could not do that, they too, were repelled by my persistent presence. I had wanted to "get the seat of my pants dirty in research," but I couldn't find a place to sit. I was quite obviously a threat to all those in and outside the courtroom, which was my cue to make a drastic change in my research setting. I wanted a setting that would allow me the opportunity to observe, interview, and casually interact with child abusers—a setting which was unique to them and in which I would present little or no threat. On reflection, I saw that I was refused access by the population I sought chiefly because I had so little advance information on the questions to which I was seeking answers, and this was apparent in the kinds of questions I had been asking; I must have seemed an indefatigable scavenger. Everett C. Hughes (1971: 497) describes this situation well:

> One who has some information and asks for more is perhaps less likely to be refused than one who has no advance information; perhaps the best formula is to have advance knowledge, but to let it show only in the kind of questions one asks.

What I was in desperate need of at the time was some information, some advance knowledge about the lives of child abusers from an "insider," someone who had been there—perhaps an ex-child abuser.

In the spring of 1973 I was hired as a child-abuse research consultant by a philanthropic foundation in Chicago. This foundation was interested in giving a small amount of seed money to a grass-roots organization in California, Parents Anonymous, that was designed to offer self-help group therapy to child abusers. During my tenure with the foundation they brought Jolly K., the president and founder of Parents Anonymous and an ex-abuser, to Chicago for a public relations promotion.

This gave me the opportunity to interact closely with her. I found her to be a woman of enormous strength and vivacity, and I was enchanted by her candor. Our meeting was a fortuitous one, for we both had needs: her need was to identify someone who would sponsor the initial efforts of Parents Anonymous in Illinois; mine was to identify a research setting where I could gather data while moving around freely and presenting no threat to the population being observed. We bargained. I would sponsor the first Parents Anonymous Chapter in Illinois to be located in Chicago with the understanding that I would simultaneously be conducting sociological research.

Although at the time I was unaware of what I had bargained for, I was hopeful that finally I would be able to interact with the practitioner, the elusive child abuser, who could provide for me data both rich and full. I would be able to do my fieldwork by observing the people in situ, which meant finding these child abusers and staying with them in some role which, while acceptable to them, would allow both intimate observation of certain aspects of their behavior and would allow me to report it in ways useful to social science but not harmful to those child abusers I would be observing (Hughes, 1971: 496).

At this point one might wonder why one researcher's story of access is necessary. Basically the point centers around an explanation of the qualitative method, which suffers derisive comments, even by many in the field of sociology. Quantitative data, as useful as they are, sometimes lack the depth and reality of qualitative information gathered through firsthand observation, as Beatrice Webb (1932: 172) noted some time ago:

> Sitting for five or six hours in a stinking room with an open sewer on one side and ill-ventilated urinals on the other, is not an invigorating occupation. But in spite of headache and mental depression I am glad I came. These two days of debate have made me better appreciate the sagacity, good temper and fair-mindedness of these miners than I could have by reading endless reports.

It is sitting in a stinking room with miners, following a detective at work, or observing "boys in white," welfare recipients, and child abusers that enables one to remark about social behavior in detail and with clarity. However, finding child abusers to study and negotiating access into their lives is not easy, and experiences previously described in this chapter point to this difficulty.

Another reason for my detailed account is to depict the tension, fraught with anticipation and anxiety, that a social researcher experiences while conducting this type of research. Many sociologists reminded me of the posture I must assume as a social researcher—i.e., to approach the respondents as if I had a *right* to the data—but only after I was actively engaged in my fieldwork did I realize that the respondents have a right *not* to give the data. Hence, maintaining access in this study became an issue of paramount importance and took a good deal of time and energy.

As mentioned earlier, the verbal contract agreed upon was that while I conducted my research I would also be engaged in the activity that I was researching, which made me a participant as well as an observer in the setting. I observed parents who either considered themselves or were considered by others to be child abusers at regular weekly meetings of Parents Anonymous. I, too, attended these meetings regularly, with my role defined as professional sponsor. (There is a detailed description of this role in Chapter 3 which deals with the Parents Anonymous model.)

My observation began early in the spring of 1973, and those observational efforts are ongoing. I was, and still am, a professional sponsor to various Parents Anonymous Chapters in the greater-Chicago area. Each chapter of the organization meets weekly on a designated evening for about three hours at a predetermined location. Some meet in park district buildings, such as the one described at the beginning of our first chapter; others meet in church basements, university classrooms, hospital conference rooms, or public school rooms. These meeting places foster anonymity, and assurance of this anonymity is something the organization takes great pains to achieve and preserve. Members share their first names and phone numbers and gather together weekly to discuss unabashedly the problem they share in common—child absue.

Sponsor: What do you think your function in the home is?

Barbara: My role in the home...that's a question mark. I really don't know. It's a dull way of life. Seems I'm always needed by one of them...and my needs are not fulfilled....Seems I'm always dissatisfied with the way things are going. I'm usually the decision maker. I think that my being a wife and mother is not satisfying enough. I'm loved by my husband but he also needs my strength. That's the most negative thing. I say unfulfilled, you know, dissatisfied, mercy! Heavens to God! If I had the strength I'd commit suicide like my mother tried to do. But then I'd miss all the misery I'm gonna have for the next 30 years.

Ellen: That's all the fun. [laughter]

Barbara: That's like me saying...a half glass of water is only half empty. A positive person would say it's half full. I'm fantastic. [laugh] I think I should go institutionalize myself!

Cathy: I feel that everything revolves around me. Ah, I am the center of the household and yet I'm afraid that something will go wrong...like when I got sick. I know only too well in the back of my mind that everything is gonna go on perfectly without me.

Ellen: I feel just the opposite. I'm just a satellite. Everyone else is the center of the universe.

Barbara: I know when I got sick everything went on without me. If I would have dropped dead that day, everything would've gone on without me. But now that I'm alive, I'm the center.

Fran: Well, that was obvious. Even though you were sick, you had the kids home for lunch.

Cathy: Remember the other day, I told you, I have all these self-imposed horrible things I've created for myself...to prove to myself how important I really am....Oh, I'm about to commit hari-kari!

Fran: It's not something that just comes overnight, you know.

Jackie: No. Like, I never heard of all these kind of things really...I got paranoid about it. When I first got married, you know, and had the feeling of having all of his family slam on top of me...you know, kidding and hugging and kissing...they do it all the time, and I wasn't used to this physical contact. And really, I'm not just running from my husband. Sometimes I think a combination of the wrong things happen....We didn't get family ties when I was growing up...we didn't get that 'one person' attention...if we got as much as a minute from a person, we were lucky! We used to go out to get negative forms of attention, too. Wherever we didn't belong, that's where we were to make sure that we were noticed.

Cathy: In the beginning I, um, felt that I had really over-extended myself. The past week when I had all this energy, I felt great. I was really 'up.' And because I was feeling badly because I had done too much, and I knew I had, it put me in a very bad frame of mind. Number one, I was very wiped out physically and unable to handle everything. So as soon as that happens, my older son starts coming home for lunch, flops the bag down, puts the fruit and carrot in the refrigerator, and says "make me another sandwich." Well, forget it! You know he comes home from school now, every day, just to check in...just to see how things are going in my squirrelly world. [laughter]

Barbara: Tell him he has to eat in school...that's it.

Ellen: Tell him you're not going to be home at lunch time.

Cathy: That's what I did today. My 5-year-old...he thinks he's ten...hasn't been coming home after school. Yesterday he was at a neighbor's house. Luckily that kid's mother phoned me to let me know he was there. She found my name and number in the phone book. Now they're not allowed outside after school. He's not allowed to cross the streets, and he was also just hit by a car. I can't trust him.

Ellen: Tell him if he comes home late the doors will be locked, and he'll never be able to get back in again.

Fran: The problem with the progression you're making is that all of the burden of decision making and responsibility stays on you.

Cathy: During the day it is. That's my role, folks! Who else will do it?

Fran: Who else? Everybody else around you! Everybody has the capacity to make a decision there. But the way you're setting it up, his punishment, and all of it, is something he doesn't have to think about at all. So he doesn't have to think about coming home because he knows that whatever it is, you're gonna figure it out and do something about it. He doesn't have to worry about coming home or his punishment or anything.

Ellen: You mean she should ignore the fact that he wasn't there, and when he comes home not mention it? Make him think she didn't miss him?

Fran: Well she's gotta give it a try. It's better than what's goin' on now, don't you think?

My role at the meetings was a dual one, and my attempt to establish my role duality in the minds of the members was an overt one. After the publicity surrounding Jolly K.'s visit to Chicago had run its course and the first members of Parents Anonymous in Illinois attended that first meeting, I explained to them that I would be happy to serve as their group sponsor but that they should be aware of my research interest. I assured them that in no way would my research efforts ever place them in a compromising position, and that I would never violate their right to anonymity or place that right in jeopardy. My silence was the price for their frankness. Initial acceptance and access were facilitated at that first meeting by Jolly K., who vouched for my professional integrity and sincerity. At subsequent meetings attended by newcomers, the "old timers" would vouch for me as I explained my intentions and my roles within the group. Hence, the absence of access renegotiation served to reduce dramatically the anticipatory tension which is peculiar to this type of research. Primarily due to the rapport I was able to nurture and maintain with the respondents, I was afforded freedoms within the setting which might otherwise have been taboo.

The use of the tape recorder was one such freedom. There were many meetings where accurately recording notes while simultaneously interacting as a participant was an arduous task. So I became facile in predicting *before* a meeting how much verbal interaction the group would require of me *during* the meeting. The indicator I used was the number of phone calls of a crisis nature I received between meetings.

As I have said before, members shared their phone numbers and first names so that if a crisis situation developed, they could reach out by telephone to another Parents Anonymous member or to the sponsor on a 24-hour-a-day seven-day-a-week basis. An increase in crisis phone calls indicated that the next meeting would be a serious one, requiring everyone's participation, including mine. This was the cue that the tape recorder would be helpful. I explained this entire process and its effect on my research to the members, and I requested—and was granted—permission to record meetings from time to time.

In most cases the members sat around or near a table of some kind. The tape recorder was placed on that table, and the agreement had been made that if at any time during a meeting a member wanted to speak without being recorded, he or she had simply to depress the "stop" lever on the machine. That option was rarely exercised by the members. It appeared that they just didn't care if they were taped by me, not only because they trusted me, but—of greater significance to them—because they thought that they were in this way helping to destroy the stigma accorded to child abusers.

I met with them at their meetings, and I responded to 3 A.M. crisis phone calls. As more rapport developed I visited them at home, and I met their children, their spouses, their relatives; I ate with them and often played with them and their children. In some cases I spent days and nights with them, all the time recording—in my mind, with a machine, and on paper—what they said, what they did, whether they hit their kids. More times than I care to remember I wrestled with the question of my right to invade their private worlds merely to gather data.

The information I had gathered, in many ways unsystematically, did not lend itself readily to codification and did not transform well into calculable form, but it did increase my skills in understanding these people's lives. And this is in keeping with the concept of participant observation, which assumes that the only true way to understand a group of people is to study them in their natural state and to gain a deep understanding of them.

Participant observation requires that the investigator adopt principles of symbolic interaction, based on the assumption that behavior is self-determined and observable at two levels—the symbolic and the interactional. Objects in the social world do not have intrinsic meaning but are defined by the individual's plans of action and are in constant flux. A consensus is reached within one's social network, and an attempt to understand this culture fully requires persistent firsthand observation. A further assumption of this method is that an individual studied as a representative sample of his or her environment yields an invalid study outside of the context of that environment. Other methods fail to produce fully inclusive results due to the abbreviated encounters with the behavior investigated; certain patterns of behavior require time to unveil themselves. The reality of a behavior is best determined by collecting the data as they occur; this method is especially useful in examining the process of change as it affects behavior and attitude, primarily due to its ongoing nature.

Garfinkel (1967) refers to this work carried out by the fieldworker who juggles roles of researcher, participant, and participant-as-researcher as "understanding work." As everyday people must try to make sense out of their daily round of living by understanding what constitutes the data of their lives—the conversations they engage in, their interactions with others—so must the field researcher make sense of his or her data to understand a general pattern. This is particularly so with conversational data, as much data collected by the researcher is accrued through conversations in which the researcher either participates or initiates. In contrast, interviewing is a more rigorous method of collecting systematized data.

From the spring of 1973 through the spring of 1975 I conducted "understanding work" while attempting to be as unobtrusive a researcher as possible. Having assumed the role of a silent, watchful observor, I was self-conscious about tampering with the data. I was careful to avoid intruding conversationally at times when I felt my intrusion would deflect the participants' attention away from themselves and on to me; yet, at the same time I wanted to interfere, interrupt, backtrack, and *direct* conversation. I had come to a point where I felt the desire to probe systematically and to make relevant inquires about these people's lives.

In the summer of 1975 I constructed an interview schedule (see Appendix), thinking that it would serve as a systematized recording of what I had observed; instead, it helped to broaden the scope of the research. I was able to obtain data not usually elicited in the group discussions—experiences that were highly personal and that had occurred prior to the Parents Anonymous experience—and data that cleared up questions about things I had observed but failed to comprehend.

The sample of 41 respondents was drawn from 11 of the 17 now existing Parents Anonymous chapters in Illinois, with over 150 hours logged in conducting the in-depth interviews. To my chagrin, the thought of being formally interviewed by me caused considerable concern among many of the respondents of the original group I had spent almost three years observing. The concerns focused on loss of anonymity, threatening questions, and, above all, the use I would make of their responses—specifically, whether anyone would be able to tell who they were by what they said. Had I not made that time investment of over two years as a sponsor with Parents Anonymous, I seriously doubt that I would have been granted the interviews.

Earlier in this chapter I described the events that led to my becoming sponsor to Parents Anonymous in Chicago and how I subsequently gained permission to use the tape recorder to assist me in collecting field notes. What I have yet to describe is the effect this method appears to have had on the respondents who made up the final sample involved in structured in-depth interviews. In considering this effect the following issue areas are relevant:

1. Anonymity
2. Rapport and threatening questions
3. "Old timers" and "snowballing"
4. Use of tape recorder as an intrusive measure

Anonymity   The major concern of the interviewees was loss of anonymity. The first respondents were all drawn from the original Parents Anonymous Chapter in Illinois because I had their confidence. I had taped many sessions of their meetings, and they had never been jeopardized in any way by my involvement with them and the Parents Anonymous group. I had kept my end of the original research bargain with them; now I was asking them to keep theirs. I assured them that they would not lose their anonymity if they cooperated in the study. Each interviewee was asked to grant me permission to tape-record the interview, and each interviewee was offered possession of the tape subsequent to its transcription. None refused to record, and none requested the transcribed tape. Their willingness to be recorded in this field research venture can be attributed basically to my role duality, which in many cases served to create instant rapport. My ability to "talk the Parents Anonymous talk" enabled me to achieve rapport with the respondents in my sample much in the same way that E. E. LeMasters's (1975) skills in playing pool enabled him to achieve rapport with the population he observed.

Rapport   Although I explained that I was conducting field research, I always prefaced my request for the interview with the fact that I was also a Parents Anonymous sponsor and understood how difficult it would be for them to discuss their child-abuse problem and experiences with me. I explained that some of the questions in the interview might seem threatening but that their responses would not be utilized in a threatening way or against them. Each time I informed the interviewees of my role in Parents Anonymous the response was positive, and they sensed that we shared something—our Parents Anonymous affiliation. The responses indicated this sensed shared unity:

> If you're with Parents Anonymous, then I guess you're okay.
>
> I'd do anything to help someone in Parents Anonymous.
>
> Long as you're not some fuckin' cop.

The rapport I had with my respondents did not make the threatening questions less so; rather, it appeared to make the act of responding a nonthreatening one.

There still remains the unanswerable question of the extent to which the rapport between the field researcher and those studied actually exists and the extent to which it is a figment of the researcher's sociological imagination. Yet the identification I felt with the respondents in my study, whether perceived or real, allowed me to complete the interviews at an accelerated rate.

"Old timers" and "Snowballing" Of the 11 chapters of Parents Anonymous sampled, I had spent time conducting field work extensively with 4, and their members were not strangers to me; however, the members of the remaining chapters were strangers, which posed a few problems in gaining access. I gained entry in two ways. First, I called the sponsors of the respective chapters, explained my intent, and asked if anyone in the group would be open to an interview. Second, after receiving first names and phone numbers of new respondents, I had them contact previously interviewed individuals who would help reduce their anxieties about being interviewed if they were anxious or frightened.

The results were favorable. The "old timers" who had developed feelings of rapport with me were able to transmit their positive feelings to the potential interviewees who, after being interviewed, became "old timers" themselves, and the "snowballing" effect was in operation. After one interviewee would explain or tell someone else in the group how relatively painless the interview was, the problem of access to members of the groups with whom I was unfamiliar disappeared. Being considered "one of them" was invaluable in my research effort, particularly the interviewing aspect.

Tape Recorder The symbiotic relationship we shared as the studier and the studied facilitated the use of the tape recorder during the interviews. For those interviewees who were members of groups where I frequently taped sessions, the tape recorder was not intrusive, primarily because they had become desensitized to it through frequent contact with it, much in the way one becomes accustomed to a heavily perfumed room after being in it for a while. For those interviewees who were members of groups to whom I was an outsider, the tape recorder was at first obtrusive and intrusive, but prolonged contact with it proved to be the key to eliciting consistent, unambiguous responses. During many interviews, in an effort to reduce tension and apprehension, I would depart from the structured questions of the interview schedule and discuss sundry Parents Anonymous matters with the respondent. I could do this effectively due to my role within the organization, and my knowledge of Parents Anonymous served to relax the interviewee. Using this technique during the interview, however, proved laborious, and many times an interview required four to five hours.

At the conclusion of each tape-recorded interview, I recorded my general assessment of the interview (see Appendix), including the location of the interview, the interviewee's manner, and a general evaluation of his or her credibility. Credibility was assessed on the basis of the consistency of each set of responses relative to every other set of responses gathered. In the interim between interviews I examined the materials of previous interviews for inconsistencies in responses, as inconsistencies had implications for the central hypothesis which was being formulated. (Briefly, the hypothesis maintained that participation in Parents Anonymous changed self-image, social functioning, and the parent-child relationship by stressing the attainment of skills in self-sacrifice, nonviolence, nondirective love, and unconditional, positive regard, and by offering its participants guidance and support during periods of skill attainment. The respondents were not told of the central hypothesis unless they requested information about it; most were not interested.) The final theory was formulated on the basis of the recorded observations of the group sessions and the interviews with the child abusers. By examining both I was able to check further for any inconsistencies in responses, which helped to determine informant credibility in the following ways: First, by observing many of the respondents outside of the context of the Parents Anonymous meetings and recording those observations, I was later able to compare what they had said and done in the meetings with the actual interview data. In the final analysis the interview data were consistent with the field notes, which not only had implications for the credibility of the respondent, but also for the theory in formulation.

I could not use this method of data comparison with those respondents whom I had observed only in the Parents Anonymous meetings; in those cases I looked for inconsistencies by comparing their responses to the responses of those whose actions I *had* observed outside of the Parents Anonymous context. Another way I assessed the data for inconsistencies and informant credibility was by comparing what the respondents said about each other and what they said about themselves. Many questions in the interview schedule required the respondent to discuss the actions of other members in the group. In a way this check on the data is tantamount to the final check on life-history data and what Denzin (1970: 249) calls the task of "internal criticism" in determining informant credibility.

An analysis usually involves the examination of something whole in an effort to determine its parts or its elements. The method I used in analyzing the data involved reasoning from the parts to a whole, or from particular instances to a general conclusion, followed by an examination of the whole for its parts. This method, called the analytical induction method, "requires that every case collected in the research substantiate the hypothesis. If one case is encountered which does not substantiate it, the researcher is required to change the hypothesis to fit the case which has proven his (or her) original idea wrong" (Becker, 1963: 45; see also Lindesmith, 1947: 9-15).

Our search for negative cases was conducted in a proper way, and we did not try to avoid contradictory evidence; however, this does not preclude some bias. We are in agreement with Lindesmith, who contends that unconscious distortion is probable in any study (1947: 9). But I must add that with respect to the central hypothesis and the available evidence, I followed certain procedures in an attempt to reduce bias. For instance, when the theory had reached its final stages, I tested it in the cases of the child abusers who voluntarily affiliated with the self-help therapy group, and then again in the cases of the child abusers who affiliated involuntarily. I contended that if the theory was valid, it would be borne out by both cases, and it was. In further search of negative cases, I compared the responses and observations that I had recorded concerning members of the self-help therapy group who told me that they *had* been abused in some fashion as children to those who said that they *had not* been abused as children. Any of these cases might have contradicted the theory; none did.

I searched the data to determine what, if any, contradictions would be provided by the respondents whose form of child abuse was soft-core in nature as opposed to the hard-core, and found none contradicting the final hypothesis. (A soft-core abuser is defined as an individual who does such things as calling the child a son of a bitch or a whore regularly and who often "over-spanks"; a hard-core abuser is defined as an individual who does everything the soft-core abuser does, only with more regularity and severity. For instance, where a soft-core abuser would use his or her hands in a physical assault on the child, the hard-core abuser might use an object such as a belt, a stick, lighted cigarettes, or cords from vacuum cleaners, coffee pots, etc.) This is significant in that much of the child-abuse literature concerned with seeking help for these individuals regards Parents Anonymous and organizations like it as beneficial to soft-core abusers but not to hard-core abusers. Any or all of the cases could have provided contradictions to the hypothesis, but none did.

The hypothesis in its final form accounts for the failure of various "rehabilitative" programs designed to change child abusers. This failure is primarily due to the emphasis on the child abusers' *rejection* of their past behaviors rather than on the *acceptance* of themselves and their past actions, which is encouraged by the self-help therapy group.

This is not a study of the motives of child abusers; rather, it is concerned with a sequence of events and social experiences which constitutes an explanation of how these child abusers changed their responses and their self-definition during their tenure as Parents Anonymous members. (For an elegant discussion on the distinctions between cause and motive, see Lindesmith, 1947: 16-17). In our research endeavor we observed people change—come of age, so to speak—while involved in self-help group therapy, and I asked them to describe that observed change in an effort to reach an understanding of how *they* defined reality. With respect to our study, however, the question of methodological weakness still remains unaddressed. Criticisms of the participant observation method concern its credibility—its bias, sample representativeness, and reliability. We are told by Miller (1971: 87); Selltiz, Jahoda, Deutsch, et al. (1959: 166-7); Zelditch (1969: 5-7); and Lofland (1971: 96-7), for example, that the most serious and pervasive element threatening the credibility of this type of research is the human element. It is the human exchange between the researcher and those being researched which arouses suspicion, and it is this human equation that is the major bone of contention. Personal involvements and loyalties to divergent groups based on the researcher's social as well as scientific dealings may produce bias. One way a researcher might protect against this would be to delimit his or her group alliances. In other words, a precautionary measure might be simply to pick a group to study and stick with it, rather than try to participate in and observe possibly antagonistic groups, such as students and administrators. Attempts to participate in two divergent groups simultaneously are met with suspicion about the covert intentions of the researcher, and often this suspicion results in stoppage of access. In my own case, my observations, although diversified at the beginning, eventually were confined largely to the members of Parents Anonymous.

Critics of this approach feel that the researcher is so close to the trees that he or she is unable to see the forest. The researcher's closeness to the respondents can be devastating to the study, to the researcher, and to those under investigation. There are no clearly defined rules for how close the participant-observer must get and for when "close" becomes too close for objective obervation; it is a research management technique that a field researcher must acquire through field-work experience if he or she is to survive in the field. While this method may appear irregular and loose, it is that very same human element earlier regarded as detrimental to scientific procedure that allows for the lifting of restraints which preclude researcher-respondent interaction. It is precisely this human factor that can draw out closely guarded feelings and beliefs all too often missed by scientific procedures mechanical in nature.

With respect to the representativeness of our sample, the questions might rightfully be raised of how and why it was selected and of what it is representative. The sample is a smaller representation of the larger whole (Miller, 1971: 55); in our case, the definition of the population making up the whole is difficult as there are no reliable estimates of how many child abusers exist. Complicating the sampling procedure even more was the problem of deciding to which group to generalize our findings. It was not our intent to generalize our findings to all child abusers, but rather to generalize to the child abuser's experience as a Parents Anonymous affiliate. And yet the exact number of Parents Anonymous groups nationwide is unknown and difficult to keep track of as they appear to spring up from state to state like dandelions in summer. In no way could we have drawn a random sample.

The essential requirement of any sample is that it is as representative as possible of the population or universe from which it is taken. We feel we have satisfied this requirement, even though our sampling method could best be described as judgmental or purposive. This type of sampling requires considerable knowledge of the subgroup selected. For over two years I interacted with four groups of Parents Anonymous that existed independently of one another, and I observed the patterns of behavior in all of them to be similar in their development. A plurality of experience and behavior unveiled itself, unlinked to socioeconomic status, age, or gender.

One of the advantages of this kind of research too often ignored is the availability of contact with nonrespondents who may never be formally interviewed but who, nevertheless, supply the participant-observer with information about the population as a whole—information that might go undetected if other methods were employed. Knowledge about nonrespondents aids the researcher in arriving at a judgment of representative sampling. Ultimately our sample was drawn primarily because of its availability, and secondarily because we did not think potential errors would threaten the basic reliability of the research.

We have covered the aspects of research as observer, participant, and participant-observer to the neglect of a type of pressure which may have an effect on social inquiry, that of the researcher as an expert. Kitsuse and Spector (1975) warn us that this

> type of pressure stems from the participation of sociologists as experts in the policy-making process...to enter the arena is to become subject to the pressures that soon lead to the abandonment of definitional questions in favor of the applied, practical, policy-oriented issues that are adjudicated there. For example, a sociologist may have researched the history of how marijuana came to be defined as an illegal drug. When called to testify as an expert, she is asked whether marijuana is *in fact* harmful to those who use it. If she is unwilling to address that issue, her expert status, whether coveted or not, will be short-lived.

Had I not experienced something similar to the example given by Kitsuse and Spector, I would in all probability have withheld any comments in this direction. But because I had aligned myself so closely with a group of people viewed largely as social garbage, and because of my liaison with a gadfly organization seeking to help them, I was asked to speak before various groups on the subject of child abuse and Parents Anonymous. This would appear to present no major problem, save for the fact that few groups are eager to hear about the adult socialization process experienced by child abusers in Parents Anonymous or about the moral career of a child abuser; what they want to know is *why they do it*. That simply was not a focal concern of my study, although much of the data are tangentially relevant to the etiological question of child abuse. But I found myself commenting nonetheless. The researcher must take precautionary measures against this happening, because the effect on the research venture may be deleterious. It requires skill to balance the roles of researcher as observer, participant, participant-observer, and expert.

Finally, I would like to touch briefly upon another matter that receives little or no attention in the social-psychological literature dealing with requisite skills of participant observations. I am alluding here to the process of canceling the research bargain after sufficient data have been gathered. The way in which a researcher moves out of the lives of the people studied can have a direct effect on subsequent researchers' attempts to move in.

3 PARENTS ANONYMOUS: WHAT IT IS AND WHO JOINS IT

During the fall of 1972 the idea for this project occurred to me. With notepad in hand, I decided to observe and interview the people involved on a daily basis in the Calendar Seven Courtroom of the Cook County Juvenile Court in Chicago, Illinois. I spent over six months in that setting, observing and interviewing the judge, the public defender, the assistant state's attorney, the sheriff's police, the clerk, and, last but most important, the people who were brought before the judge for adjudicatory hearings. The people in legal jeopardy were suspected child abusers.

In Illinois, as in many states, if it can be demonstrated, let us say, by a social worker that a parent has the potential to commit a physically abusive act against a child in his or her care, then that demonstrated potential is sufficient evidence to warrant the legal recommendation of foster care placement for that child. It is at this juncture that the people previously observed in a state of legal jeopardy turn into people facing a life crisis situation which they are un-prepared to meet and ill-equipped to handle. Families in jeopardy become families in crisis. The crisis is not that their child has been taken away from them, but rather what they must do so that the child will be returned to them. What to do, now that they have been called child abusers?

Question: Could you recall the experience?

Response: Of being told that I was a child abuser? There were several...the case workers know about all of them. But they only had one particular incident to base their accusations on. I'm not sure it was really an incident. The little girl, Terry, had gone to school with a cut lip. The teacher asked her how she got that. She said, mommy pushed her on the stairs. I really don't remember doing that particular thing.

33

The school called the agency. The agency got involved and came out the same day and pulled the kids out...in a very awkward way.

Question: How?

Response: They kept Terry at school. I was frantic because she didn't come home on the school bus. When I called the school and talked to some secretary there, she said, "Terry is here." I said, "What's she doing there?" She said, "Someone from the agency is here too, and they want to know if they can come over and talk." At that moment I knew something was going to happen. They did come over. She said they were going to take the kids out. They had told me what had happened. I said I didn't know if that's true or not. I don't recall it as being true. They said, "How could you not know what you did?" I couldn't remember that particular thing. I said, "Can't you give me a couple of days with them and say good-bye properly?" They said, "No, we're just taking them." "Is it okay if my husband comes home from work and can say good-bye to them?" "No." They had the van outside already and drove the kids out with all their stuff. The case worker after that was working with me about once a week. We weren't getting too much accomplished, though. "What's going to happen? How will this go down on the record?" She replied, "There would be suspicion of abuse on your part." It was the first time I had ever really thought about it.

Question: What did you do?

Response: When the kids were taken away, I went into a very deep depression. I would close all the curtains to keep the light out and I would lock myself in the house...having a few drinks during the day, which isn't something I would ordinarily do. (Interview #5)

Question: Why was she [your child] taken out of the house?

Response: She had fallen from the slide; she was in Children's Memorial about four days. I kept here there because people had said it was the best hospital for kids. I didn't realize that they were such sticklers on child abuse. Otherwise I wouldn't have taken her there. Then she had bumped her head, most likely, on the bars of the crib. She was too old for those things that go around. Some intern put down that she fell out of the crib. That's when everything started.... They called a case worker. He talked to the doctors, he talked to social workers at Children's Memorial, to me, to Brandt, to my parents. He asked my parents if they would adopt Chrissie. My parents really got mad because they didn't want to see [her] taken away from me. Why should they want to adopt their own granddaughter? (Interview #18)

Question: I would like you to tell me where you were and try to remember what you were doing when you first felt that you had a problem with coping with the children or that you had a problem with child abuse.

Response: Well, let's see...when I first started noticing when my son was only a year old when we moved here....He's hyperactive and I don't mean that as a cop-out...the kid is very active and he has a problem. Sometimes he don't sleep for two days, and he gets into things, and I noticed that I'm screaming at him all the time....Now with my 7-year-old, I enjoyed raising him. That was a lot of fun...but Robbie, I've felt that he was out to get me at times....It wasn't too bad until September....My husband and I are separated, and I went to live with my father....I had an abortion during the time I was gone....I found out that I was pregnant, and we just decided there was no sense in having the baby. I kind of flipped out and...because of my own personal problems with the abortion and the marriage, I was taking it out on Robbie....I was yelling and screaming and watching him all the time with a "what-are-you-going-to-do-next?" look. I yelled at him and screamed at him all the time, but it didn't seem to bother him, and then one day he laughed at me while I was screaming at him, and I started slapping him in the face, and I knew then that something had to be done. Once it was 4 in the morning, and again he wasn't sleeping, and he kept saying that he wanted a drink of water. So, I'd get out of bed, and as soon as I'd get in his room, he'd say he didn't want it, and he wouldn't drink the water...."I want a drink of water, I want a drink of water," he'd say; so finally, I just said, "You want the water?...Here, I'll give you water!" So I threw the glass of water in his face....That scared me, so I called the child-abuse hotline, and I said, "I'm afraid I'm going to hurt my kid," and they gave me the P.A. number, and I called them right away....(Interview #28)

Question: First of all, I would like you to tell me if you can recall where you were and what you were doing or how you were feeling when you first felt that you had a problem with child abuse.

Response: Oh, that's a hard question. I guess I've always...maybe I think I just didn't identify with it or that I had the problem until, I'd say, after my divorce....My son was around 3 when it started, I think.

Question: What started?

Response: I felt very frustrated....I missed my kids, who were in foster care, and I didn't know if I wanted them back, you know. I didn't understand the rejection of my "ex" and my divorce, and I couldn't handle it, and I talked to my mother every day for two years about how I was a failure....I felt, what did I do wrong? (Interview #32)

Question: Could you tell me where you were and what you were doing when you first suspected that you were a child abuser?

Response: I was at home. What had happened was, I neglected to put the children in the proper care when I take off somewhere. It became a habit...not really caring who had the children just as long as somebody had.

Question: Did you start having negative feelings about yourself?

Response: Not really. I thought I was doing what was best because by law they require the children are not left alone, that they are in somebody else's care. I felt I was doing what the law required.

Question: When you would leave the children, would it be to go to work, to shop, or what?

Response: Well, the first incident was that I left the children with some people upstairs, and then I called a girl I grew up with in the same institution who [now] has a heart problem. She needed some help. So, I ran upstairs and left the children with these people and told them that I would be back in a couple of hours. I went over to help this girl. By the time I come back, I was told that I was under arrest....My apartment had backed up and the toilet had backed up. They were trying to claim that the children were in the apartment at that time, which they weren't. This is when I realized I had a problem.

Question: What kind of a problem did you think you had then?

Response: Well, things were going through my head...was I a good mother?..was I doing something wrong?..how could I get help for this? The pressure of the kids was kind of great on me. I have an epileptic baby, and I am an epileptic, and it's hard to give attention to two children when you have a hyperactive son and an epileptic one. It was just a lot of pressure, and I asked for some help and I didn't get any.

Question: Who did you ask to help you?

Response: I asked my visiting nurse for some help. I told her I needed help because I felt I was losing all values around the children, since this.

Question: Why did you talk to her and not [ask] someone else for help?

Response: Well, she was the only person at that time that I felt I could trust. It turned out to be the opposite. She was against me instead of for me.

Question: Did she report you?

Response: Yes, she did.

Question: Were the children taken away from you?

Response: The children were taken away after the [toilet] incident. I had received them back three days later and then they were taken away again.

Question: What was that visiting nurse's response to you when you told her you needed help?

Response: She said, "I can't help you, the kind of help you need." I told her I was having very many problems with myself and I was really confused about what was going on. I was never raised in a home. I raised myself. I didn't know how to raise children...I still don't...but I'm learning. I did not know what to do for the children or anything.

Question: How did her response affect you? When she said, "I can't help you," how did that affect you?

Response: It hurted me because I haven't asked anybody for years for any help because I'm the only person...I'm the bad person. I felt I trusted her enough after working with her for a year and a half that at least she would try to give me some help. Or if she couldn't, she would try to find some agency that would. When she told me she couldn't, and she won't try because she didn't think it was her problem, it hurted me. I felt very bad. I knew that in the long run something with the children would happen, and they would get taken away. I knew that, because I just couldn't work with the children, I couldn't do anything right.

Question: How did you come to have this visiting nurse?

Response: I really don't know. I was pregnant with the first one when I came upon her. I was very sick in my old apartment, I nearly died of double pneumonia. She came up and she stayed in the apartment that I was in for a week until I was well enough to go to a clinic. This is how I got her.

Question: What kind of suggestions did she have for you? Did she make any suggestions to you on how to handle the children?

Response: She told me that I needed to put my children in a foster home. And that I needed to get away from them. She felt that I shouldn't have the children. Period. And I told her that I was not going to give the children away. I thought it was awful, you know, I figured I had friends that kept their kids and I wanted mine.... (Interview #17)

From these interviews it is apparent that the child abuser's problem is neither relieved nor eased when the child is removed from its natural environment; instead, removal of the child only serves to intensify and magnify the problem within the abuser. It is also quite apparent that the state agencies conveniently ignore this situation by defining the child as the problem-victim in most cases, instead of defining the child abuser as the victimizer with a problem. Defining the issue in these terms allows the state agencies as well as the judicial system to embark on a course of action which involves amassing support systems and reinforcements for the child in lieu of doing anything constructive and supportive for the parents—the victimizers with a problem. As the system rallies around the child, the parent with the problem literally walks out the courtroom door.

As all these thoughts began to take shape along with my research interest in child abusers, I had the good fortune to meet Jolly K., president and founder of Parents Anonymous.

PARENTS ANONYMOUS

The literature distributed by Parents Anonymous states that it is a crisis intervention program set up to help prevent damaging relationships between parents and their children. The Parents Anonymous approach based on the self-help concept claims three major advantages over other more traditional, nonclient-centered, directive forms of therapy. First, it claims that it gives parents with a child-abuse problem an opportunity to share their feelings with other parents experiencing similar problems. Second, it claims that because the group leader or chapter chairperson is always a parent with "experience of abuse" ("experience of abuse" refers to having been abused or having abused someone), a group member can identify with him or her more readily and in a way that is not possible with a professional therapist, whose "experience of abuse" is deemed vicarious at best and voyeuristic at worst. Third, the organization claims that the assurance of anonymity affords the parents involved in Parents Anonymous the opportunity to express their feelings and to discuss their abusive actions without risk of public disclosure and the accompanying social recrimination. Members of Parents Anonymous are only asked to share a first name and a telephone number with other members of their chapter. The organizational literature of Parents Anonymous contends that through participation in a Parents Anonymous chapter, parents improve their self-image which, in turn, improves both their social functioning and their relationship with their children.

The organization of Parents Anonymous further postulates that child abuse involves two factors: the *abused* and the *abuser*. It is the contention of Parents Anonymous that abuse is the outward manifestation of the abuser's problem but not the problem itself. It is the claim of Parents Anonymous that the beauty of the self-help therapy approach lies in a chapter's ability simultaneously to encourage and prod parents into talking about their problems, i.e., themselves.

The organizational model appears to be based on a model of child-rearing which excludes emphasis on directive control while emphasizing:

1. Self-sacrifice
2. Nonviolence
3. Nondirective love
4. Unconditional positive regard
5. Guidance and support

It is the belief of the organization that this model of child-rearing embodies the ideal or socially prescribed parental role.

BASIC RESEARCH QUESTION

The major research goal of our study was to determine how participation in a Parents Anonymous Chapter changes self-image, social functioning, and the parent-child relationship. An ancillary goal was to determine whether the basis for the organizational model is, in fact, the previously described one; and if it can be demonstrated that it is, then how the proposed model of childrearing is made operational by the organization and its members. The implementation of nonabusive childrearing is of singular importance, since Parents Anonymous proposes that skill development in the five areas listed above changes self-image and social functioning as well as the parent-child relationship.

Before it is determined whether the basis for the organizational model is as described, an analysis of the model is helpful. The following points will be considered:

1. Composition of group membership
2. Provisions for entering and leaving group
3. Division of labor
4. Group mores
   a. Function of secrecy
   b. Negative sanctions
   c. Ritualism
   d. Distinguishing members from nonmembers
5. Group preservation
   a. Morale
   b. Control of behavior
   c. Recruitment

COMPOSITION OF GROUP MEMBERSHIP

In considering the group membership composition we looked at the characteristics of the respondents within our research sample. Since we will be depicting many of the characteristics in percentage form, we feel their description lends itself best to tabular presentation (Tables 1-13).

Table 1
Composition of Group Membership
by Sex and Race

Female	
White	92.6%
Black	4.9%
Male	
White	2.5%
Black	0

(N = 41)

Table 2
Formal Schooling of Respondents

Less than high school	17.5%
High School graduates	42.5%
College graduates	35.0%
College +	5.0%

Table 3
Composition of Group Membership by Age

16 - 20	0
20 - 25	20.0%
26 - 31	47.5%
32 - 37	25.0%
38 - 43	5.0%
44 - 50	2.5%
50 +	0

(N = 41)

Table 4
Composition of Group Membership by Religious Affiliation

Protestant	37.5%
Catholic	15.0%
Jewish	7.5%
Eastern Orthodox Christian	2.5%
Nonaffiliated	32.5%

(N = 41)

Table 5
Composition of Group Members by Employment Status and Occupation

Employed out of home	
Office/clerical	32.5%
Factory	5.0%
Nurse	7.5%
Teacher	5.0%
Student	5.0%
Chef	2.5%
Employed solely in home	31.9%
On welfare	10.6%

(N = 41)

Table 6
Employment Status of Respondents' Spouses

Employed	
Blue collar/factory	50.0%
White collar/office	33.4%
Unemployed	16.6%

(N = 30)

Table 7
Number of Children in Family

1	25.0%
2	47.5%
3	10.0%
4	10.0%
5	7.5%

(N = 86)

Table 8
Status of the Family

Mother, father, child(ren) in home	65.0%
Mother and child(ren) in home	30.0%
Father and child(ren) in home	0
Child(ren) not at home, in foster care	5.0%

Table 9
Marital Status of Group Members

Married	67.5%
Unmarried	
Divorced	25.0%
Unwed mother	5.0%
Widow	2.5%

Table 10
Duration of Marriage* of Those
Married or Once Married

Years	
0 - 5	52.5%
6 - 10	25.0%
11 - 15	12.5%
16 - 20	5.0%
20 +	—

*Present or most recent marriage.

Table 11
Parental Status of Respondents' Spouses

Spouse/father of children	64.1%
Ex-spouse/father of children	17.9%
Father unknown	12.8%
Spouse in house not father of children	5.2%

Table 12
Number of Times
Respondents Married

0	5.0%
1	70.0%
2	22.5%
3 +	2.5%

(N = 41)

Table 13
Age and Sex Distribution
of Respondents' Children

Male	71%
Female	29%
Less than 6 months old	0
6 months to 1 year	3.4%
1 to under 2	6.9%
2 to under 3	8.1%
3 to under 4	15.1%
4 to under 6	16.2%
6 to under 9	20.9%
9 to under 12	16.2%
12 to under 15	8.1%
Older than 15	4.6%

(N = 86)

It is plausible to conclude that the "typical" child abuser could be best described as:

Caucasian
Female
About 30 years old
Protestant
High school graduate
Secretary, housewife, or teacher
Married only once, a little over 10 years
Has a couple of young boys
Husband about 30 years old, works in a factory or office

This would, however, be an imprudent conclusion, based on insufficient, inadequate, and inappropriate data. What has been neglected in this stereotypical description is the person's definition or preception of himself or herself and its congruency or incongruency with his or her location in society. As we look at the composition of a group's membership we are asking implicitly, what kind of people join this group and what kind of people don't? The answer would allow us to draw inferences (although imprecise) about members and non-members. For instance, we might infer that those who belong either want to, need to, or have to and that those who don't belong don't want to, don't need to, or don't have to. But we cannot use only the available characteristics of our respondent members as direct indicators of what kinds of people abuse their children; that is, we cannot say that most child abusers are typified by the attributes listed earlier. However, the list does allow us to say something about the kinds of people who either voluntarily or involuntarily become involved with Parents Anonymous because of a problem with child abuse. We can also comment on previous research in this area.

Earlier we mentioned that the individual's self-definition has been widely neglected by most studies. It should be emphasized that even with this sparse data, strong and direct conclusions have been drawn too hastily regarding people who have problems with child abuse.

For example, most of the studies of child abusers (see Bibliography) have been concerned with causation, i.e., why some people abuse their children and others do not. The child-abuse literature is replete with descriptions of life-style models that appear to provoke violence against children by their caretakers. In an effort to satisfy questions regarding cause, life-style models are created in lieu of attempting to ascertain whether the practitioner's definition of an activity or life-style is consistent with the onlooker's. The child-abuse literature to date seeks to define the activity by categorizing it demographically while excluding the practitioner's definition of the activity. By ignoring both this and the practitioner's feelings and looking only to the activity itself, we are misled with regard to the meaning and implications of the activity. The unfortunate result is that while we end up assigning people to a social category, we neglect looking at the person's framework of imagery for judging himself, herself, and others, which he or she *shares* with others by virtue of a common membership within the designated social category. This makes it difficult to determine what kind of people compose the membership of this social category. Failure to derive the practitioner's definition and description of an activity can lead to inaccurate conclusions concerning those people who engage in the activity. Let us illustrate:

Question: What did you think other Parents Anonymous members would be like?

Response: I was afraid they would be beneath where I was...they were going to be illiterate and maybe a little less than human...just not have all the deep feelings I did...much more brutal than I was. (Interview #4)

Response: I thought their intelligence would be really down and they weren't like me. They were grubby people. I thought they were probably scum people and I don't want to have anything to do with them. I didn't really consider myself a child abuser. Maybe deep down, inside, when you know something but never come out and verbalize to anybody. I thought they were different from me. (Interview #11)

Response: I thought that I was probably going to be better than them. I was really surprised. I thought that they would be lower income people from the poor sides of town. Probably had their children in the hospital several times, and that kind of thing, which wasn't true at all. (Interview #12)

Response: I thought they would be very violent people...the type I wouldn't want to associate with. (Interview #13)

Response: I thought they were low-income, low-educational types. (Interview #15)

Response: I was frightened of them. (Interview #18)

Response: I thought I was awful, you know. I figured I had friends that...I used to go to their house and I'd see their boy with a black eye, big knots on his head, broken leg, broken arm, you know, and it really bothered me, but I couldn't report them...I couldn't let myself 'cause it's a good friend of mine, you know, I just couldn't turn them in...couldn't...I think it's really bad...I never do that to them [my kids] to really hurt them, you know. Just like I had a girlfriend that lives downstairs from me...the one downstairs from me and another girl are the only ones that knows what really happened and they won't stand out, which I think I would, you know, but I can't because I wasn't there...I just heard hearsay...you know, a little baby went to the hospital...it was a couple of...two weeks ago it went to the hospital or something and...it had plywood in the back of its head....When it happened the mother come down the hall to get this other lady to come up there and she turned around and said, "Oh, my God! My baby, it's dead, pick it up, it's dead," you know. And she took the plywood off it's bed and put it behind her....See, the reason that she had put it [the plywood] on there, she said, is because she liked to sleep late in the morning, so she and her husband took the plywood and put it on the [top] baby's bed...it's [the baby's] height, you know, and the baby got its neck caught between the bars in the baby bed, and it had tried to get out of the bed, and I guess it brushed its head up against the plywood. It's a year old and it was dead on arrival to the hospital. And she's the one that killed it, there's no other way you can look at it. Her and her husband both....That really bothered me when she was telling me about it. It's awful the way people are, and it's really stupid because a lot of people from child-abuse agencies...people that come out to check you out to see if you're really beating your kids...they will go to somebody's place where really there's not much really going on to their kids, where they let these other people get away with murder, you know, and that's what really freaks me out. I think that's awful and they haven't done anything to this lady, she's really...she's a young kid...she's 17 years old, and I heard she did it because her boyfriend said he was going to leave her and she told him if he left he'd never see the baby Jeremy, that was his name, again. And I guess that's the reason she did it. But you know she heard the baby choking, she had to. Probably took it two or three hours to do it to itself you know. And a baby when it's choking or it's hurting its head or anything...it's going to scream like crazy. It was a real small apartment so she had to...she had to see it.

Question: How do you feel about her and her story? She's a child abuser.

Response: I feel real sorry for that baby and that young kid mother. Nobody helped them. I don't understand. Why couldn't those child-abuse people do nothing? I just don't understand. (Interview #30)

Thus we have the image—a group of low-income, low-educational, frighteningly brutal and grubby people engaging in frighteningly brutal and grubby activity called child abuse—an image which not only permeates the minds of persons interviewed for the purposes of our study but also the literature on child abuse. For example, Banfield (1967: 53-4) comments on the lower class and violence:

> The lower-class household is usually female-based. The woman who heads it is likely to have a succession of mates who contribute intermittently to its support but take little or no part in rearing the children. In managing the children, the mother, or aunt, or grandmother is characteristically impulsive: once they have passed babyhood they are likely to be neglected or abused, and at best they never know what to expect next. A boy raised in a female-based household is likely at an early age to join a corner gang of other such boys and to learn from the gang the "tough" style of the lower-class man.
>
> The stress on "action," risk-taking conquest, fighting, and "smartness" makes lower-class life extraordinarily violent. However, much of the violence is probably more an expression of mental illness than of class culture. The incidence of mental illness is greater in the lower-class than in any of the others. Moreover, the nature of lower-class culture is such that much behavior that in another class would be considered bizarre seems routine. In its emphasis on "action" and its utter instability, lower-class culture seems to be more attractive to men than to women.

The dangerous supposition in Banfield's comments is that the provocateur of violent actions is the lower-class fatherless household. Again, inappropriate subjective correlations are put forth.

In his book *Violence Against Children* David Gil (1970: 6) defines child abuse as

> the intentional, nonaccidental use of physical force, or intentional, nonaccidental acts of omission, on the part of a parent or other caretakers interacting with a child in his care, aimed at hurting, injuring, or destroying the child....

From this definition we would infer that practitioners of this activity intentionally engage in it with the aim of harming the recipient of the actions. Here we must point out that the data used to support this definition were derived from the following sources: a series of studies that included a nationwide survey of public knowledge, attitudes, and opinions about physical child abuse, conducted during October 1965; nationwide press surveys of child-abuse incidents during 1965 and 1967; a pilot survey of child-abuse cases in California reported between September 1965 and February 1966 to the State Department of Justice; a survey of every incident of child abuse reported through legal channels throughout the United States in 1967 and 1968; and an analysis of every incident reported through legal channels during 1967 in a sample of cities and countries. For all the sophistication of this epidemiological study of child abuse, the following question must be raised: How is it possible to derive a functional definition of child abuse based on newspaper clippings and public attitudes? In addition we ask: Solely on the basis of newspaper clippings and public opinion attitudes, how can the intentions of the practitioner of an activity be determined and interpreted?

As previously discussed, most studies of child abuse and child abusers have been concerned with causation and definition. I, too, am concerned in our study with causation and definition; however, I am more concerned with ascertaining whether there exists any discrepancy between the explanations of causation and definition as offered by previous research and the practitioner's explanation of the same.

The stereotypical description is useful, however, in that it puts into empirical question the findings of previous research that foster myths which correlate race, sex, age, religion, marital status, occupation, and education with violent activities, and specifically with child abuse.

Sex and Ethnic Group   Specifically, and of significance for future research, we found that over 90% of our sample were Caucasian and female, which places in jeopardy the notion that child abuse is taking place predominantly in a "dark ghetto" where action-oriented males are the major perpetrators. We are aware that our sample was not drawn on a random basis, and it is not our intent to generalize to all generalizations drawn by previous researchers.

Educational Status   In contrast to the findings of previous research regarding educational status of child abusers, over 40% of our sample were high school graduates and 35% were college graduates. This is in sharp contrast to Gil's finding of only 16% who were high school graduates and only 0.4% who were college graduates. Given our figures, it would be in error to assume that high educational levels and child abusive actions are mutually exclusive or, on the other hand, that there is a direct relationship between low educational levels and child abuse.

Age of Parents Although 67.5% of our sample were under 31 years of age, the average age of parents was 31, which does not support the observations of previous studies which indicated that the parental age was extremely young. The average age of the respondents' spouses was 32.0.

Religion While 60% of the sample expressed a religious affiliation, this figure is significantly lower than the approximate religious distribution of the entire population as reported by Gil* where almost 95% expressed religious affiliation. We feel this figure indicates a need for more research examining relationships between religious indoctrination and attitudes of violence as well as violent behavior. Additionally, our sample yields over 30% with no religious affiliation whatsoever as compared to the 3.5% figure, again reported by Gil, representing no affiliation for the entire population.

Occupational Status The occupational status of the parents in our sample corresponded to their educational level for the most part, with 57.5% of the mothers in the labor force working mostly at white collar occupations. Again, our figure is significantly higher than the 39% of working mothers in Gil's study.

Over 80% of the respondents' spouses in our study were employed, in contrast to a figure of a little over 50% of the males employed in Gil's study.

Number of Children The proportion of families with four or more children was nearly twice as high in Gil's sample when compared to all families in the United States; in his sample 37% of the families had four or more children and 21% had two children. The national figures used by Gil (1970: 110-11) reveal that 20% of the population have four or more children with 30% having two children.

Referring to Table 7 we see that 17% of our sample had four or more children, which corresponds closely to the national figures; and while 47% of our sample had two children, which is somewhat higher than the national figures, we find that 72% of our families had one to two children, which compares to 62% of the national population of families with children under age 18. National percentages (1957

---

*The religious distribution of the 1967 sample cohort corresponded rather closely to the religious distribution of the United States population as reported in 1957 by the Bureau of the Census. Sixty-two percent of the sample cohort were Protestants and other non-Roman Catholic Christians, 25.5 percent Roman Catholics, 0.7 percent Jewish, 1.8 percent other religions, and the affiliation was unknown for 10.1 percent. The approximate religious distribution of the entire population is as follows: Protestants and other non-Roman Catholic Christians, 66 percent; Roman Catholics, 26 percent; Jewish, 3 percent; other religions, 1.5 percent; none or not reported, 3.5 percent. (Gil 1970: 107)

Census) further indicate that 37% of United States families have three to five children, which is a little higher than our figure of 28%; however, our figure corresponds to the national percentages more closely than Gil's figure of 57%.

Family Structure Based on his findings about the structure of the families in his sample, Gil suggests an association between physical abuse of children and deviance from normative nuclear family structure. We feel that our figures put this suggested association into question. Among our families, 65% consisted of the mother, father, and child(ren) living together in the home (as opposed to the 46% figure of Gil), and of that 65%, 86.6% of the males were the fathers of the children in the home. Of the families in our sample, 30% were composed only of the natural mother and her child(ren), which strongly correlates with Gil's figure of 29% for this category. Although our figures on marital status correspond, our strongest departure from Gil's percentages is the difference in the number of fathers living in the home with the mother of the children. Again, we would suggest, that our figures weaken the argument that there is a strong association between physical abuse of children and deviance from normative nuclear family patterns.

Sex and Age of Children Referring to Table 13 we see that the age distribution of the children of the families in our sample is not limited to very young children under three, as has been suggested by numerous investigations. In this category our figures correspond to Gil's.

We concur with Gil's opinion that the findings of many earlier studies in child abuse were biased. The bias in the selection and the composition of the groups studied resulted, perhaps, because the studies were conducted in medical settings where the more severely injured victims are seen.

But we also find bias in the selection and composition of the group studied by Gil. His sample consists only of reported incidents of child abuse and therefore is also a selective segment of the child-abusing population. Gil has no data on those families where abuse is not reported officially. This is where we find our sample to have utility, since it includes both families whose abusive practices have been brought to the attention of the local and state agencies and families whose abusive actions have never come to the attention of law enforcers or child-welfare agencies (i.e., 35% of the members are self-referred). Thus we can present and empirically support an aspect of the composition of a group of child abusers heretofore neglected: those who define *themselves* as child abusers. We are referring specifically to the self-definition and self-perception of child abusers who belong to Parents Anonymous.

Question: What did being a child abuser mean for you?

Response: It meant I was miserable; I hated myself. I was abusing myself. I was doing that all my life up until the time my child was born and then there was just someone else there to abuse along with myself.

Question: Being a child abuser meant being miserable?

Response: Yes.

Question: Could you tell me a little bit more about that? What did that mean—being miserable in comparison with other people you knew and thought you knew something about [referring to an earlier response]?

Response: Seeing other people sure of themselves and confident. They were sure of what they were doing, they knew what they wanted to do, and they went ahead and did it. I never even knew what I wanted to do. I was...no matter what I did, I was always uncertain as to whether I did the right thing. I never knew what the "right thing" was. It was always pummeled in my head that you aren't suppose to do bad things. And everything that I did I interpreted it as being bad. (Interview #1)

Response: It means that I [slight pause] hit my kids. I want to find a way to stop hitting them. To understand them better, love them better. Any way I can find to help me do this I'm all for. (Interview #2)

Response: Child abuse is when a parent is acting a certain way towards their child that's detrimental towards the child physically or emotionally and it's happening all the time. It's something that the parents can't control. It's a constant thing that goes on every day. The parent has no control over what they say or what they do. They can't break their negative patterns. They may even know they exist and know how terrible it is but they can't do it by themselves. (Interview #4)

Response: It meant that I had a problem which was more than just overly disciplining them...it meant that my life wasn't changed. I found it very hard to get up in the morning. I couldn't face it. Sometimes there would come a rush of love and guilt and hatred for myself. But the patterns would still exist. The negative things that happened would still exist. There were times at night, especially when I had been extremely physically hard with them, that I would just lie down at night and cry. Just cry. Not for them...cry for me. I felt that they were doing terrible things to me, that the four of them were very strong personalities and they were trying to crush me. I couldn't stand up to the children. (Interview #4)

Response: It meant practically that I was some sort of a criminal. I was just about the worst person you could think of...I just took a big guilt trip about the whole thing. I did have and still do have nightmares about the things I did to the kids. I would think to myself, how could you possibly do such things? I think that if I weren't put down as a child, I would have a better self-concept. I think if as a child I were made to feel basically okay, I would want to make my child feel okay. Since I was raised to think that I was not okay, I have no basis to give my child an okay feeling. (Interview #5)

Response: Well, it's very hard to get up and say "I'm a child abuser." I mean, that it is a very difficult thing to do. It took me a long time even to admit it to myself. But now, I've recognized it as a problem. It's a problem that can be cured. It's a problem that has hope. It's not devastating or anything like that. I'm growing, I'm *not* so much the material mother as I was before. There have been improvements in just the year that I've been to Parents Anonymous.

Question: Did you find yourself fitting into that description of child abuser? You had mentioned earlier that they're horrible creatures. Do you find yourself fitting into that description?

Response: Oh, yes, I would beat them. I would use the belt. My main problem was belittling them, doing the same thing my husband was doing to them. Making them feel less than nothing because I felt less than nothing. It was just like a chain reaction, you know. When I recognized what I was doing, I did feel horrible about it. (Interview #7)

Response: Like being a mother was something I didn't know how to do...how do you find out how to do it?...How do you make a decision and then take responsibility for it? How do you know whether it's right or wrong? Well it takes practice. Believe me, it takes practice. It's rote work. You don't learn how to give a shot to someone after you've done it the first time. You practice on an orange, you practice on a grapefruit, you practice on an arm. It takes a while. But after a while you develop the technique; you know how to do it. It's no different...learning to be a parent. Only thing is you don't start out a little bit at a time...you get a kid, the whole ball of wax your first time out...and I don't know how to do it....What does being a child abuser mean for me? It means I'm a flop!'' (Field Notes, October 1974)

Question: What did being a child abuser mean for you?

Response: Before or after [Parents Anonymous]?

Question: Both.

Response: Ah...before it meant really physical abuse...I mean beating a kid, screaming at them constantly, just in general...neglect, and now...neglecting the kid, you know, letting him lie around in dirty diapers for days, or not feeding him. Now it means not only physical abuse but mental abuse...like I still holler at Peter a lot of times when I'm...well, I don't really think I should, or I take out my anger on him, angered at something else, and I transfer it to him and I yell to him about it. (Interview #26)

Question: What did being a child abuser mean for you?

Response: A little sad...to realize that I could really hurt the kid, to know that...I thought I was going crazy...or was it my mental attitude towards him, or was it just my mental attitude towards myself, you know, I didn't know. When I would scream at him, use obscene language, which I really shouldn't do, because he really don't know what you mean, and hitting him so hard, sometimes...I just continuously punish him...I don't only just punish him once and just let it be, I just continue all day with the same thing, and one day I hurt him really bad, and I realized that I was a child abuser...I threw him on the couch, one day. You see, I couldn't find my car keys, and I'd left them down so he could play with them, which I shouldn't have done if I was going to go somewhere, and I had to be at the store that was going to close, and I asked him where my keys were, and he didn't answer me, so I picked him up and threw him on the couch again....Once on a Saturday afternoon, I remember that I was so mad at my little boy, after I had spent all day to clean up my house because Steve's parents were coming and because my mother-in-law is a "white glove" cleaner, and I wanted everything to be really neat. And I would be in one room and he [my boy] would be in the other [room] messing up the one I had just cleaned. I think the last straw was when I went into the bathroom. He put toilet paper in the water and just threw it [around]. And I had the whole bathroom to clean all over again. Then I got mad at him. I shook and hit him so hard that I had bruises on the back of his arms and back, and I thought that if I would do something like that to him, I need somebody to help me. That's what it [being a child abuser] means to me. (Interview #24)

The critical component in group composition is not the numbers of children the child abusers have, or their educational level or occupational status but, rather, what kind of people *they* think they are and how *they* feel about themselves. What kind of people are they? They are people with a strong sense of self-worthlessness. More than suffering because they abuse their children, these individuals suffer an attenuated sense of self. Their feelings of inadequacy, self-contempt, and dejection come to full fruition when faced with the adult life crisis of parenting. Perpetual failure is the major theme of their lives; they enter marriage, parenting, and the job market with failure all around them. Due to the ubiquity of failures in their own lives and in the lives around them, there is no one from whom they can learn how to succeed—no one consistently and continuously successful around them to imitate or emulate, and they become convinced of their own worthlessness.

Traditionally this attenuated sense of self has been associated with members of the lower class. And since the discipline of sociology proposes that psychic states are influenced by location in society, it has heretofore been accepted as logical by social researchers that the lower one's station in society, the less of a positive self-image one is likely to have. We find this to be especially prevalent in the juvenile delinquency literature. For example, Eleanor Pavenstadt's study of lower-class childrearing patterns notes in the discussion of "very low lower-class" families that the "saddest, and the outstanding characteristic of this group, with adults and children alike, was the self-devaluation." (1965: 92) Konopka (1965), in her study of several hundred delinquent girls ranging from 13 to 19 years of age in Minnesota institutions, concluded that the girls had a poor self-image and added that their complex identity problems were aggravated by their low-income culture, which defined the female status as inferior and undesirable. In the 1943 study of 530 clinic-treated prostitutes, Kemp found the women were socially, medically, and psychologically "below par." We hear more about this "futility syndrome" in the *Roots of Futility* (Polansky, Borgman, and DeSaix, 1972), which is a study concerned with childhood levels of living and childrearing patterns in Appalachian culture. Polansky et al. report the ubiquity of alienation, desolation, isolation, and apathy, to name only a few attitudes ever present in a culture of lower-class status whose value system "does not include wall-to-wall carpeting."

What we are trying to illustrate here is that there appears to be an attempt by social researchers to establish positive correlation between feelings of self-worthlessness and having lower-class status in our society. We question this notion that a poor self-image is a class-linked characteristic. To this end we find our previous description of the child abuser who joins Parents Anonymous to be invaluable. Most of these people are hardly of lower-class status and the average educational attainment would hardly indicate illiteracy. Yet they are parents who traumatize the children in their care; and they are parents who—in the legal sense of the word—abuse, and who are providing an environment injurious to the welfare of the child(ren) in their care. As a result of our findings we concur with Liebow's assumption (1967) that people will fit into various roles regardless of their social class. Being a child abuser involves performing a role based on perceptions of a role identity; our point is that perceptions of abusive-role identification are not class-linked characteristics. The myth that child abusers are low lower-class types who *intentionally* harm the child(ren) in their care, as Dr. Gil would have us believe, is just that—a myth.

The fact that poverty settings provide ease of access for data gatherers is all too often ignored. The slum is not a place of concealment, where one can beat one's child and attract little attention; rather, it is a place of inescapable containment, as opposed to the middle- and upper-class "ghettos," which offer concealment and redefinition of activities.

Specifically, an injury inflicted on a child nonaccidentally becomes, more often than not, redefined as accidental in emergency rooms frequented by middle- and upper-class patrons. One of the factors greatly influencing this pervasive process of redefinition, we feel, is the idea that an attenuated sense of self is both the provocateur of deleterious social functioning and a class-linked characteristic; therefore, deleterious social functioning is expected of members of the lower-class, but not of members of classes with superior socioeconomic status. Further, we would add that social science must share the responsibility of promulgating the notion that self-worthlessness is a class-linked characteristic as evidenced in the literature previously mentioned. It is also reflected by the plethora of studies attempting to uncover the self-perceptions of lower-class members of society as opposed to the paucity of work done in the area of self-perceptions and social functioning of the middle and upper classes. This is particularly true in the case of middle- and upper-class child abusers. Our data indicate that a person with an attenuated sense of self, a child abuser, is a role people may fit into regardless of their social class.

Now let us consider Eliot Liebow, a person held in high esteem by this social researcher. In his classic *Tally's Corner* (1967) he described "Negro streetcorner men" as illiterate, unskilled, and convinced of their own self-worthlessness due to their experiences with a multiplicity of failures, but he went on to say that their goals were really no different from those of the rest of society. However, their failure to achieve even a modicum of success with respect to those goals forced them to seek the sanctuary of the streetcorner where the failures they would elaborate beyond reasonable proportion were easier to bear than the reality of incompetence, and thus they could face tomorrow.

Like Liebow's "streetcorner men," the child abusers in our study seek the sanctuary of Parents Anonymous, where repeated failures can be elaborated so that they, too, can face tomorrow.

Question: What is it about Parents Anonymous that makes it a helping thing?

Response: Well...I've had for a long time this terrible feeling that I wasn't put on the earth for any specific reason, and whatever it was it would be quite better if I was removed from the earth and that my life wasn't much...but then there was one session with Jolly K. when she was here and it was said that you do deserve a rich and rewarding life, and they asked me to say it, and I couldn't 'cause I didn't believe it and they said, say it anyway. It took quite a while before I could even say it, and then this man said, when you go home tonight, make a sign and put it up some place, like on your mirror on your dresser. And I've got the sign there, but I don't say it every day, but I do think it...nothing has helped until I've been to Parents Anonymous. (Interview #21)

Response: It's a place where people can talk about their problems openly without feelings that they will be judged, or put down, in any way. (Interview #23)

Response: Nobody cares if you're married, single, or if you're happy, they're just there to listen, to express how they feel, to get ideas, never put you down, or anything. It changes the way you feel....I think the biggest change is the way that I feel about myself. I use to hate myself horrible, I thought I wasn't worth two cents, that my husband deserves someone better than me, my child deserves someone better than me. And through the talking that I did and the listening that I did, it's made me feel better for myself. Feeling good about myself has made me feel good about my family. I'm really a pretty decent person. (Interview #24)

Response: Just the fact everyone in the group really seems to care. I have never been in a group that after just a few meetings, everybody was, you know, unhappy if I couldn't come to a meeting or happy to see me, and when I was out for awhile, almost everybody wrote me a letter, you know, to say what was happening and that they missed me, and they hoped that I could come back, and it was kind of fun. Well, I think that's unique. (Interview #26)

Response: Being able to go to the meetings, some time to get out, it's fun. Also, we trade babysitting back and forth. There isn't too many people at the meeting that I wouldn't give my kids to. We usually just abuse our own children, and we're more tolerant of other people's. I got out, I got a friendship, and it's gone on since then. (Interview #12)

Response: I think that it is a safe and secure place for people to go...I think it's a place where girls can complain and talk about the problems that they have with their children to other mothers who are there, because they have similar problems, hopefully, anyway, and that to make them feel that their children are a little more normal and not the big monsters that perhaps they might have thought they were. (Interview #20)

Response: It's helped me to direct the problem I did have—that I do have. It's helped me to cope with things better. I know when I'm having a battle royal over here [at home], I can pick up the phone and there's somebody there that will give me the support and the help that I need. I've realized that I was feeling guilty for my son's hyperactiveness and P.A. brought up the point that it wasn't my fault [that he's that way]. There's no reason for me to feel guilty but I was treating him special. Better...well, not better than the other children, just special. I would not leave him home, I would take him with [me] to prevent arguments. Because I was doing this that was making him [a] special child in the family...and P.A. helped me recognize that I was not helping him at all. It helped me a lot, like I say, with my son more. It helped me to cope with a lot of his ups and downs and in-betweens. He's becoming a normal child again. I quit treating him special. He's recognized this. He's fulfilling his thing of the inner child. (Interview #7)

Response: I think in the biggest way it helps, first of all, to be able to go somewhere and talk about your problems. That's the first thing. Because I never really was able to discuss the problems that much even with the psychiatrist because he kept going back to my past life more than the future or the present. I think that the other big thing that you know in P.A. is that all these other people have these problems like you have had or are having the problems at the time. And if you call one of these people, you know that they're going to try to help you in some way, give you an alternative to your anger or whatever. You know that these people are going to listen to you because they really want to listen to you...even in small things. There are a lot of small things that I call people about. In fact, even my sponsor. I would've felt a lot of my friends would wonder why I would be calling them [about] something that was small. But to me they were big things. They were really serious things to me. (Interview #10)

Response: What is different about P.A. is that it isn't afraid to get personally involved with you. And I think that the therapy group I was in and the individual therapy I had was all this noninvolvement on the part of the therapist. They don't want to get involved in the personal life you have. If you're in trouble after 5 o'clock in the afternoon, well, too bad for you. In Parents Anonymous there is a whole lot of personal involvement. If you need somebody to be with you at your house for a whole day at a time in the beginning, somebody from the group will be there. If you're having a hard time in the middle of the night with your kid, then you call somebody in the group at 4 A.M....It's that personal involvement you can't get anywhere else. (Interview #1)

PROVISIONS FOR ENTERING AND LEAVING THE GROUP

Parents Anonymous groups have few provisions for entering or leaving the group. Plainly and directly it is assumed by the organization that a person goes to a Parents Anonymous meeting because he or she has a problem with child abuse. Anyone with the problem may enter the group. There are no fees, dues, or records kept on any member. During the period of membership, each member is encouraged to attend meetings regularly, and each member is expected to observe the prerogative of all Parents Anonymous members to remain anonymous both during and subsequent to their membership. If a member at any time chooses to drop out of Parents Anonymous, he or she may do so without relinquishing the right to return to the group. This is clearly indicated in *I Am a Parents Anonymous Parent,* the handbook that every new member of the group receives.

On Dropping Out...And Coming Back In:
If you've dropped out of Parents Anonymous for a while, for whatever reason, don't worry about saving face if you want to come back. Don't agonize over what everybody must think of you for not keeping in touch, or all those things that don't matter. Just come on back in. Everybody backslides now and again. Just remember, if you want to be here, we want you here. Welcome Home. (*I Am a Parents Anonymous Parent,* 1974: 18)

DIVISION OF LABOR

In looking at the allocation of special tasks to different strata of individuals in Parents Anonymous, we find that each Parent Anonymous Chapter consists of members, a chairperson who is a parent member, and a sponsor who donates his or her professional time to the chapter.

The Chairperson:
The chairperson, like you, has had, or still has a child abuse problem. He or she has been chosen by the members to be the guiding force of the chapter, and that role is an extremely important one to you and the other group members. If members show lack of support for the chairperson, then the chairperson's role as leader is undermined, this could very easily destroy the chapter's effectiveness and ability to work together as a close, cohesive group. This in no way means that members may not disagree with the chairperson, nor does it mean that every member should like the chairperson. Quite the contrary. Parents Anonymous wants and expects members to talk freely and openly about disagreements they may have with the chairperson, the sponsor or other members—but we want you to air your feelings in a constructive way. (*I Am a Parents Anonymous Parent,* 1974: 15)

The Sponsor:
The sponsor's role in the group is to help the chairperson to be a strong and effective leader. The sponsor assists the chairperson and is a "backup resource." Sponsors are a big help when it comes to training the chairperson in group techniques (lay therapy), answering questions that the group can't otherwise find answers to, and in locating other resources in the community. (*I Am a Parents Anonymous Parent,* 1974: 16)

GROUP MORES

When we speak of mores we are referring to rules and customs backed by severe punishment. In the context of Parents Anonymous we are looking at its mores as "the required behaviors." There are quite a few of these, and they are clearly spelled out in the handbook. Parents Anonymous has divided these behaviors into two categories: Guidelines of Achievement and Guidelines of Allegiance.

GUIDELINES FOR ACHIEVEMENT

1) I will recognize and admit to myself and to other Parents Anonymous Members the child abuse problem in my home as it exists today and set about an immediate course of constructive actions to stop any further abusive actions in my home.

2) I want and accept help for myself and will follow any constructive guidance to get the strength, the courage and the control that I must have in order that my child(ren) will grow up in a loving, healthy home.

3) I will take one step, one day at a time, to achieve my goals.

4) I may remain anonymous if I desire, but I may identify myself and at any time call upon Parents Anonymous members or seek constructive help before, during, or after my problem of child abuse occurs.

5) I must understand that a problem as involved as this cannot be cured immediately and takes constant working within the Parents Anonymous program or other constructive guidance.

6) I admit that my child(ren) are defenseless and that the problem is within me as a parent.

7) I believe that my child(ren) are not to be blamed or subjected to my abusive actions regardless of what the cause is.

8) I promise to myself and my family that I will use, to the fullest extent, the Parents Anonymous program.

9) I admit that I am alienating myself from my children and my family, and through Parents Anonymous I will make myself the center of reuniting my family as a loving, healthy *family unit.*

10) I admit I must learn to control myself, and I do these things in order to achieve harmony in my home and to earn the love and respect of myself, my family and society.

GUIDELINES OF ALLEGIANCE

1) I, as a member of Parents Anonymous, will always respect the anonymity of fellow Parents Anonymous members.

2) I, as a member of Parents Anonymous, will always promote a true and honest understanding of Parents Anonymous and the problem of child abuse, and will help fellow members and society to better understand the Parents Anonymous program.

3) I, as a member of Parents Anonymous, will never suggest that we have the total repsonsibility or the total answer for the rehabilitation of the person with an abuse problem.

4) I, as a member of Parents Anonymous, will never suggest that any form of abuse is more harmful than another form or that any member is more abusive than another.

5) I, as a member of Parents Anonymous, will never judge, condemn, or make light of another person's problem of child abuse.

6) I, as a member of Parents Anonymous, will always remain supportive to other members and persons with child abuse problems in their struggle to overcome their problems.

7) I, as a member of Parents Anonymous, will always extend a helping hand to any persons who express a desire for our help with parenting difficulties.

8) I, as a member of Parents Anonymous, will never deny help because of race, color, creed, national origin, religion, economic status, form of or severity of abuse problems.

9) I, as a member of Parents Anonymous, will never attempt to coerce, threaten, or harass another person into involvement with the Parents Anonymous program, and instead will use the methods of invitation, attraction and encouragement to reach out to troubled parents.

10) I, as a member of Parents Anonymous will always uphold the Parents Anonymous concept, Guidelines for Achievement, and the Guidelines of Allegiance.

In reviewing these mores and also the few provisions for entering and leaving the group, we find identity concealment to be a very strong function of secrecy. Secrecy and identity concealment of members in Parents Anonymous is generally believed to be essential to the group's welfare and its continued existence. Parents Anonymous stipulates that it is out to help child abusers and not to punish them. By offering its members assurance of anonymity, Parents Anonymous protects "its own" members from agencies and institutions whose mandate it is to report incidents of child abuse and punish the offenders. Actually Parents Anonymous provides asylum for child abusers. It offers sanctuary to those who would seek it out.

A member may relinquish that anonymity or protection of identity at any time without gaining or losing status within the group, but there are strong *negative sanctions* with respect to anonymity and recidivism.

> Parents Anonymous will never tamper with your right to remain anonymous.
>
> The two exceptions to this rule of anonymity are first, when a member chooses to disclose his or her anonymity and/or participate in television, radio, magazine and newspaper interviews, speaking engagements, and other public appearances. Even then a member may still maintain anonymity if they so wish and so indicate.
>
> The second exception is in regard to a member who continues abusing to the degree that such behavior could result in injury or death to the child. Under these circumstances, the Parents Anonymous privilege of anonymity is being abused, and we cannot and will not condone a mockery of Parents Anonymous goals and the Parents Anonymous program by providing the cloak of anonymity to the person who continues this degree of abuse. Our goal is to *stop* our abusive behavior. Child abuse has killed and continues to kill and injure children. Should there be a member in your chapter who is in this position, the chairperson and sponsor are expected to help that member put a stop to his or her behavior *before it's too late*—for both the child and the parent. (*I Am a Parents Anonymous Parent,* 1974: 14)

Although there is a strong negative sanction with respect to recidivism of abusiveness, the violation by a member of another member's right to anonymity is one of the few actions, if not the only action, that can result in total ostracism of that member from the group.

Question: Have you ever had to kick anyone out of the group?

Response: Yes, there was one person that was kicked out of the group...I still have contact with her. I felt that it was a game that she was playing with us and her game was such that she was trying to be thrown out to prove how bad she was. There was really some good underneath and she really needed the help....We talked about it, but the rest of the group felt that she could be a threat to them and to their children being taken away. She eventually had to leave. (Interview #4)

Question: Have you ever or has your group ever had to kick anyone out of the group?

Response: I don't ever remember anyone being kicked out. I remember a couple of people had been told that you're not doing what you came here to do—what's the sense of you wasting your time coming here? And if they weren't willing to start putting things together again, they just stopped coming.

Question: What did you think led up to that?

Response: Led up to be told this? The fact that every week they came back saying the same things—saying they know what they're supposed to do but they're not doing it. The whole purpose of being in P.A. is to "do" it; to use these alternatives; to change what you're doing...with something you like better...and when someone doesn't use alternatives they are reprimanded.

Question: And when someone doesn't use alternatives and they are reprimanded, how is that carried out? And who usually does it?

Response: Well, it depends on who's in the group. It may be anyone in the group...it depends on who's in the group. (Interview #1)

Response: I remember it was one new member. She jumped on me. It had to do with my husband. She took his side. A little is coming back. But I don't remember the exact incident, but I remember she attacked me and that she thought the whole thing was all my fault.

Question: Did the attack have anything to do with the fact that this particular problem that you were raising had no bearing on Parents Anonymous meetings?

Response: It depended on how you looked at it. Our particular group met and we discussed many things. Abusive parents is one thing we talked about...there are reasons why they are abusive. There are other causes for their frustrations and that leads up to abusive parents being abusive. Until you clear up that outlying stuff, you're only going to wind up with the same crap. You say to youself, "OK, I'll try to be better to my kid, and I'll try to control myself," but you're not getting to the exact problem of relieving that which brought on the abusiveness and that was her premise.

Question: That your problem with your husband was not related to the problem with your children?

Response: She felt that we were only to talk about children problems at P.A. because that's how they did it in Michigan where she was a member. That was her reasoning. I remember that she completely

64

sided with my husband. It was really the wrong way to go for another P.A. member....I resented her for the fact that she didn't try to help me and support me.

Question: Have you ever or has your group ever had to kick anyone out of the group?

Response: I think she dropped out by herself. The people were not understanding of her because she really wasn't looking for help for herself. She was looking to be patted on the head and have someone say that she was really a good mother and doing the best that she could. (Interview #6)

Question: Have you or any member of your group ever punished or reprimanded another member?

Response: I recall this person with the job. I remember speaking harshly. You tell the person so many times and they don't go out and do it. You find yourself speaking harshly to them, in a harsh manner, not really meaning it. To punish them. It's just that you really care about them. Not just because you want to hurt them. But you want them to know that you mean what you say and it might improve their lives sometimes. (Interview #11)

Question: Have you or any member of your group ever punished or reprimanded another member?

Response: Yes...the situation was the friend who introduced me to Parents Anonymous who had really interfered to the point where I couldn't stand it. She was causing problems for other members in the group. Not that she meant to, I don't think she could help herself. She was told to leave the group. I felt very bad about it. I didn't see that there was any choice in the matter.

Question: Could you describe what led up to that ousting? And how it was carried out?

Response: It was the interference and the problems she had caused for other people plus what she was giving to me. The interference was so great that we as a group could not function because we were afraid to open our mouths.

Question: What was the fear about?

Response: The fear that the woman was opening her mouth to people in authority. It was hurting other people. Something had to be done about it. (Interview #17)

RITUALS

> Ritual is strongest when it is most perfunctory and excites no thought....Ritual is something to be done not something to be thought or felt. Men can always perform the prescribed act, although they cannot always think or feel prescribed thoughts or emotions. The acts may bring up again, by association, states of the mind and sentiment which have been connected with them, especially in childhood, when the fantasy was easily affected by rites, music, singing, dramas, etc. (Sumner, 1959: 61)

If when we speak of ritual we are referring specifically to a procedure involving a regularly repeated, traditional, and carefully prescribed set of behaviors intended to symbolize a value or a belief, then Parents Anonymous groups are devoid of ritual. On the other hand, if we approach ritualism in its most general sense as adherence to a prescribed form of behavior, we find that ritual does indeed exist within the groups we observed. For example, a new person coming into a meeting is encouraged to tell his or her story and share with the group a little of his or her background.

Question: What do you talk about at your Parents Anonymous meetings?

Response: If we have a new person come in, we go through the story of their background, but then, after a while, everybody knows you and knows what goes on. So we say, "How was your week last week?" and talk about incidents that come up that you found it hard to handle or got you really upset. We talk about what that person did in that situation. What they could have done instead if it was an unhappy situation. We talk about the good things we've done, or what we learned. We set goals for things to do in the future that we'll say next week. Then we come back and report how it changed, or if it was good. Or to see if it's working. The same things don't always work for the same people. You have to try several things. (Interview #15)

Response: Well, the first thing when you go in, you tell your first name, and we ask if anyone has an extra special need or problem that they really need to talk about and we go to them first and they'll tell us the problem; it'll be like, how awful the kids have been like this week, or what you did to them. (Interview #13)

Response: They listen and they really care...it's unbelievable. I do bring in problems sometimes which I really can't handle then, and when I leave their meetings, I can handle them. I walk out of these meetings and feel like I've said it at least...I'm sort of drained but I'm relieved....They give me great ideas there, and I just come back and I am thinking about them and I write them down and I usually do them...I usually do them [apply them] right away...and if it doesn't work I'll work with something else, you know...but it really works. If I really felt that I had a heavy problem during the week, I usually write it down; of course, I usually don't forget it, but I usually write it down, and I usually sometimes read my problems because it's hard to talk about them, and then they give me the feedback....First there is this silence, and then the people are thinking it bothers me because it's very uncomfortable, and I figure that maybe they just don't know what to say but the thinking of thoughts....They use different alternatives, too, for the meanings....This is a good example. One time when I was going to school I was very nervous raising my hand and volunteering information, and they said we should work on some alternatives....The sponsor said, "I'm going to write everything on the board that I think in writing, and all of you do the same thing and tell Carolyn what she should do before she goes to school next time." They said for me to take a bath, rest, take a nap, and so on. They wrote down all these things and it came to about 50 things, even though some of them didn't make much sense to me....The sponsor said I should talk to myself about these suggestions, read them over, and see which things I would prefer to do before I went to school. Do you know that it really worked? I went to school and I had no problem at all. That's what's so special about this group...there are no time limits on how much time a person can take up, and they really concentrate on your problem. (Interview #32)

Response: We talk about the husbands because a lot of them doesn't want the mothers to call them, you know, because they feel that it's all a big waste of time...that it doesn't mean anything, you know, their going to P.A....that they're going to nothing and stuff like that....Lots of the husbands feel that way, and then they're jealous and that's because they feel that Parents Anonymous is helping us where they can't get that same help, you know....We talk about how a parent can set up a situation and it turns out to be a bad situation for the parent and the child, but the parent sets it up so that it turns out that way or a...how kids do certain things to test a parent out and they're just testing, but it's just like a game for a child to see how far he can push mommy or daddy. (Interview #30)

When engaging a prospective new member at a group meeting the old members *encourage* the prospective member to reveal the information that serves as his or her credentials for membership; this could be referred to as an activity that approximates ritualism in Parents Anonymous groups. Aside from this encouraged performance, at no other time is a member *expected* to perform a specific task.

Question: During the first time, was it communicated to you what was expected of you if you joined?

Response: No, not really. I was made to feel comfortable. I remember that.

Question: How?

Response: They just made me feel comfortable. They didn't look down or prejudge. I found myself having their problems and if they had a problem I felt it was mine. (Interview #3)

Response: You couldn't pull any punches.

Question: What was expected, and who told you?

Response: Mainly, the sponsor and the other people in the group. What was expected was that we were to be honest and truthful in telling our stories and telling about ourselves. To be honest—as honest as we *could* be. (Interview #4)

Response: Well, I don't think anything was...that's why I liked it. They never said, "We expect this of you." They were all very nice people. When you feel inferior anyway and you don't like yourself, when some people pay some attention to you, and you think they really mean it, it means a lot. These people were asking me quesitons, getting me phone numbers and saying, "Call me sometime." No one had ever done that to me before. With family...I had nothing like that. Some of them I was kind of leery of....The more times I went, I think I trusted them a little bit more. I was very afraid that they were going to tell somebody—the sponsor, the chairpeople, I thought they were going to go to Children and Family Services or something. So, I didn't tell for a long time what I had done. I just said that I don't like being a mother. Finally, I said, I can't stand this any more, I have to say this. (Interview #9)

Distinguishing members from nonmembers is virtually impossible. For example, members are not obliged to display stickers on the rear bumpers of their cars or to pass out pamphlets to individuals or to welfare agency affiliates unless they choose to. There is absolutely nothing that says a Parents Anonymous member must be distinguishable in any context unless he or she voluntarily wants to relinquish anonymous status. Because some persons who join Parents Anonymous fear what the legal authorities would do to them if they were discovered and legally labeled child abusers, and because some of the members *came* to Parents Anonymous after having had dealings with the welfare and legal systems, assurance of anonymity is a key tie that binds and preserves the existence of each group.

GROUP PRESERVATION

Still another key force in preserving the group's existence is the feeling that "it's us against them;" or "it's the lay people against the professionals." There is a notable distaste for professionals, who are seen as impersonal, uninvolved outsiders who threaten to invade the members' lives without permission or notice. The professional is viewed as a model of detachment who withholds his or her emotional self from the client, patient, or any other person in a subordinate position. It is the collective orientation of Parents Anonymous that fosters common values in personalized attachments and attentions.

The common value instilled in each participant is one having to do with the importance of *people* rather than the importance of *things*. (Leonard Davidson alludes to this very issue in his paper "Counter-Cultural Organizations and Bureaucracy: Limits on the Revolution," 1975.) It is this personal interaction that is the Parents Anonymous hallmark. It is the promise that someone really does care that keeps members participating and entices nonmembers into wanting to become members so that they, too, can share in the familiar warmth promised. It is the personalization of service to those who seek out those services that augments individual morale; this in turn affects the morale of the group in a positive way.

Question: If you were to compare or contrast other groups that you've been a member of to Parents Anonymous, what would you say is unique or different about being a member of Parents Anonymous?

Response: I think, first of all, that's confidential. It is. I don't think anybody goes around broadcasting what goes on, or anything like that. I think that because it's a family, kind of a family group, you just don't go to a meeting and forget about it for another week. You're constantly in touch with people during the week, if you want to be. Usually, with other groups, there's a meeting, and that's it. See you next week. And that's all. And with this, you can keep in touch with people, and not just a one night thing. (Interview #9)

Response: Parents Anonymous is a very warm and caring group, and it's that caring feeling, the work that is there, that they really care about you, that made me come back. (Interview #21)

Response: I felt like I was in a family....It's safe, it's like what goes on there stays there....It poses no threats....They give me the support, give me affection that I never had from my mother....The idea of holding a woman's hand or having anybody touch me in any way really turned me off. These people taught me to know the warmth of another person's hand or having somebody's arm around your shoulder. Or, being able to literally cry on someone's shoulder and have them take you in their arms and just let you cry on their shoulder. (Interview #13)

Response: Well...I know I go to a psychologist and I go mainly for myself, not for my problems with my son and I, but I think I have accomplished more at Parents Anonymous, and I like it when, well there's people, you kind of feel like everyone's got similar problems...there's some kind of tie with everybody, you know...it's closer and everybody can talk...it's more than just a one-to-one thing, you know, and it's really great...talking mainly about the problems that you've had all day, and sometimes we get into things that go deeper, of how we feel about ourselves and I don't know...but mainly it's just like what happened during the week and how we are going to work on things to make them better and try to get along with our kids.... (Interview #37)

Response: I guess it's just that everybody tries to help each other out and give them their ideas...you really get a lot of ideas and it helps...that's what really helps. At first our group wasn't that close, and so then we had to talk about everything. If you have problems you can call each other....I don't like calling the hot-lines because I don't like to talk to people that I don't even know....I've never did that and I wouldn't like to do it....Even my kid can call up the sponsor if he needs to talk to someone about how bad I'm being, and they'll listen to him, too! You call someone up on the telephone and they help you with exactly what's bugging you right then and there instead of trying to put you down or hurt you or something. (Interview #39)

Response: The people. They care. I have never run across a group like these people....I mean, friends can care, but it's different with P.A. people...they just don't try to pacify you and say that it's going to be all right...if they feel that you're wrong, they'll tell you, "Hey, I don't think you're leveling, I think you're copping out, I think this is wrong." You don't always get this from friends, and you don't get the "you're wonderful" bit from P.A. people, either....I mean, it's like they don't always like what you do or say but they like *you*....It's a very honest group...they give you a feeling of real support...it's helped me...I know it's really helped me. (Interview #32)

CONTROL OF BEHAVIOR

Earlier we mentioned that Parents Anonymous groups are "collectively oriented," meaning that decisions are made with the good of the group in mind. It is the collectivity composed of individuals which must survive and be preserved.

When we speak of a collectivity, generally we are referring to any aggregation of persons who consciously share a set of common values and who, by virtue of this conscious sharing, feel somewhat bound to one another. It is this symbiotic relationship that sets collectivities apart from groups who, by definition, engage in social interactions but are not necessarily bound to one another by shared values. The operation of social control in groups and in other collectivities differs as a result of differences in the systems of interaction (Merton, 1957: 299).

Since it has already been established that the system of interaction within the Parents Anonymous collectivity is an informal and personalized one, the control of behavior is dealt with and accomplished by personal involvement and informality.

Basically Parents Anonymous seeks to control behavior in two areas by decreasing child abuse in the home of the Parents Anonymous member and by improving the self-image of those members. Since these two areas are the foci of our discussion with respect to the moral career of a child abuser in Parents Anonymous, we will comment only briefly concerning them at this time.

It is the claim of Parents Anonymous that although it cannot cure everyone, participation in its program *can* improve the self-image, which in turn will enable a parent to rear the child(ren) in his or her care nonabusively. The organization further claims that curbing the deterioration of the parent-child relationship and replacing negative reactions with positive reactions will improve the self-image and act as a catalyst in promoting comfortable social functioning. How much of this is accomplished is related to the informal system of controlling behavior operative within the collectivity. We submit that the changes occur as a result of responses by individuals to the stimulus of the collectivity.

For example, Parents Anonymous offers what it terms "positive behavior alternatives" in what they call a "do-it-now" approach to alleviate critical parenting problems. The deterioration of the parent-child relationship is curbed when replaced by these "positive behavior alternatives."

> *Using and Giving Alternative Suggestions:*
> Let's face it, you can't get very far in achieving your goals if you're not willing to try new ways of behavior and to share them. Sharing is the backbone of Parents Anonymous—group sharing of positive methods along with group support to carry through with these suggestions will help you to develop positive behavior patterns. (*I Am a Parents Anonymous Parent*, 1974: 17)

The ways that these alternative suggestions can be shared are not as numerous as one might think. While they may be discussed at the regular weekly Parents Anonymous meeting, behaviors in need of change also occur prior to and subsequent to these meetings. Parents Anonymous has provisions for such occasions should they arise.

Each member is strongly encouraged to share his or her telephone number with everyone else in the group so that the lines of communication among the members will be open. It is assumed that these lines are available to all members on a 24-hour a day, 7-days-a-week basis. In addition, members are encouraged to use the phone as an "alternative" to abuse. In other words, "Pick up the phone *instead* of abusing your child...and if you don't call us, we'll call you as evidence of our concern and supportive reinforcement for your attempts to achieve change."

Members are encouraged to seek each other out via the telephone exchange system and also by visiting each other and exchanging such services as baby-sitting for each other's children during stressful times. All of these activities are defined as "alternatives to abuse." All of these operations are also descriptive of kin-based network activities; the majority of parents who are members of Parents Anonymous in our sample have kin in relatively close proximity, but such supportive kin-based network operations are virtually non-existent. With the establishment of the surrogate family tie, the Parents Anonymous members receive the advantages of familial support, reinforcement, and sanctuary, without the disadvantages of formal familial controls. Rather, the controls are informal ones, offered supportively, which stimulate self-reinforcing behaviors. To illustrate:

Question: In reading some of the Parents Anonymous literature in the little blue book...the little blue pamphlet, I've noticed and I've run across the word "alternative." Could you tell me what that word means?

Response: Well, gosh, it's a different way of doing what you have been doing, such as, well, a real good example is my little boy got some Desitin and smeared it all over his dresser and himself and his clothes and I was really mad, you know. I don't know what I would have done before but I do know what I did now. Instead of yelling at him or hitting him or something, I picked him up and put him in his bed and closed the door and called one of the girls from the group and screamed at her. Then I went back in and cleaned it up and changed his clothes. You know, it was over. The alternative for me was that instead of screaming and hollering at him and telling him that he was really bad, which I normally do, was to call somebody while I was mad instead of beating him or something. (Interview #31)

Response: I think that now, when I start getting to the point where I'm gettin' really bad...I can feel it coming on...it kind of creeps up on you, I would call someone and, say, I'd talk really bad about the kids. But they understood. I'd go..."I, I hate them, I can't stand them. I'm leaving, I'm leaving." And they go, "Right, right. I know you do hate them." I'd go, "You're right, I do." By the end of the conversation, "Well, I have to go, the kids and I are going to go." You're saying, you hate your kids. Oh, it feels so good to say it and have somebody say, "Right now, you really do. There's nothing wrong with that." (Interview #15)

Response: Alternatives...there are several alternatives, what the child's behavior is like can get you feeling ghastly enough for you to feel that you're going to strike a child. You can either remove yourself or you can call up somebody and say, "Would you come over and get my kid for awhile?" so that I can pull myself together or at least until I have a chance to talk about it.

Question: Do you use alternatives?

Response: I have found myself saying, what else can I do but hit them? And I do think of things to do, and then I don't hit them. (Interview #21)

Question: Do you talk about alternatives to abuse at the meetings?

Response: Yes. For instance, instead of screaming at the child or hitting him or something, a good alternative, at least for most of us, seems to be, to put the child in the room and tell him, when he's getting over whatever it is that has made him mad...it's only if it's his fault, then he can come out and rejoin the world, rather than if he is behaving badly, to just beat him or holler at him or something.

Question: So you use these alternatives to abuse?

Response: Yes, yes. (Interview #26)

Response: Well, another alternative would be to, if you feel that you've got to strike out, you go in the bedroom and shut the door and you just play it away at the mattress, just to get that physical anguish out of you, your body. Now, I don't know if I use the word 'alternative' so much, but as I described my changeover from being a parent of physical identity to handling the situation...I used an alternative of change into a rational way of dealing with child problems rather than the physical way.

Question: Do other members in the group use alternatives?

Response: Yeah.

Question: How do you know?

Response: I get phone calls all the time.

Question: Do you feel that the parents who use alternatives experience change?

Response: Definitely.

Question: Could you elaborate on that for me?

Response: We have a person in the group right now who came to our group six or eight weeks ago. Instead of beating her children she used to beat on herself...she would hit herself with her fists. She was bruised up when she came to our group. But now she goes and beats out her frustrations on her bed or on the floor or something instead of herself or the kids.

Question: As an alternative?

Response: That's what I mean by an alternative. (Interview #23)

The respondents in our sample agreed unanimously that using the telephone exchange system, visiting members during the week, exchanging varied services with Parents Anonymous members, and simply attempting to adhere to the values of nonviolence set forth by Parents Anonymous made nonabusive child rearing a reality for them. Their patterns of social functioning were altered by developing skills in these areas.

RECRUITMENT

With regard to growth and size we must keep in mind that this organization sees itself as an alternative to what the bureaucratic system at present offers to child abusers. Thus in a very broad sense this organization wants to change society. However, in order for more people to be reached and more services provided, the organization must grow. This kind of growth and expansion requires the selection of persons on the basis of special competence in a variety of areas; but the bureaucratic forms that growth inevitably introduces are seen as undesirable by Parents Anonymous

This places the organization and its longitudinal future in a precarious position. As Kanter (1972: 148) points out, "it is impossible both to satisfy individual needs and to work toward the collective good."

In considering the various aspects of the Parents Anonymous organization we found the answers to our basic research questions which we presented in the earlier segments of this chapter. We found that the organization's operational definition of successful and nonabusive parenting included self-sacrifice, nonviolence, nondirective love, unconditional positive regard, and guidance and support. An operational definition consists of a description of particular procedure necessary to produce the desired effect; it is a detailed set of instructions. (For an in-depth discussion of operational definitions, see Blalock, 1972: 2-15.) What members acquire during their affiliation with a Parents Anonymous group is a knowledge about and skill development in these processes and how *much* of these ingredients or elements are necessary to produce nonabusive parenting and a positive self-image through experimentation and the counsel of others.

LIABILITIES OF THE PARENTS ANONYMOUS PROGRAM

As I have mentioned before, secrecy and identity concealment of members in Parents Anonymous are believed to be essential to the group's welfare and its continued existence, but they are also it's Achilles' heel. Identity concealment, which we found to be a very strong function of secrecy within the group, impedes members from making their parental progress readily known to social workers, physicians, probation officers, etc., with whom they may also be coming in contact during the time they are members of Parents Anonymous. We have found this to be a major problem with the program. By offering its members assurance of anonymity, Parents Anonymous is protecting them from agencies and institutions whose mandate it is to report incidents of child abuse and to punish the offenders; but in assuring that anonymity it also prevents its members from communicating to agencies and institutions their change, their growth, and their progress. Although Parents Anonymous does provide asylum and sanctuary for those who seek it, it makes it difficult for members within the group to relinquish that anonymity for positive and constructive purposes. I have said that theoretically, if members relinquish their anonymity, they don't risk losing their status within the group; but in fact they often *do*. Time and time again I observed dissension, tension, unrest, and paranoia among group members when an individual member chose to relinquish anonymity, let us say for example, to a social worker. The relinquishment of anonymity sets up a dynamic which is detrimental and destructive to the group process. I would like to illustrate this with an example.

Let us assume that an individual member in the group may choose to communicate with her (his) social worker that she (he) is involved in Parents Anonymous and would be willing for the social worker to establish contact with the group's sponsor, who in many, if not most, instances would be a mental health professional. The social worker and the sponsor of the group then attempt to interact concerning the progress and status of the parent while she (he) is involved in Parents Anonymous. But it is extremely difficult for the professional sponsor to share information with the social worker, mainly because there is no documentation of a member's progress: there are no records or files kept on individual members, nor are there regularized reports. Interviews and group sessions are private and there isn't any really "shareable" information available, as there is in the traditional professional community. This situation creates blockages which impede effective communication between and among professionals dealing with the individual parent and/or family. When the parent becomes aware of this situation and of the fact that communication between the professional sponsor and the social worker is dysfunctional and counterproductive to her (his) goals, she (he) begins to resent the group, the sponsor, and the heretofore cherished anonymity. This situation is akin to wanting to "come out" (among homosexuals) and not being able to do so because of the deleterious effect it may have on the rest of the group. The extraordinarily strong group orientation in Parents Anonymous makes it difficult for individuals to find their self-identity during periods when they are growing and wish to share that growth with others like themselves and with professionals with whom they are coming in contact.

Another effect relinquishment of anonymity has on the group process is the paranoia most, if not all, of the group members feel. Unlike the member relinquishing anonymity, they are unprepared to relinquish their's at that time. This paranoia derives from the possibility that the member who decided to relinquish anonymity may either accidentally or purposefully reveal the identity of someone else in the group. For example, let us assume there are two parents in the group who abuse their children with similar frequency and severity. Let us further assume that one of the parents is involved with the social welfare system and has a social worker who makes home visits from time to time and who interacts with the parent while the parent's children are in foster placement. Again, let us assume that the other parent is not involved in the social welfare system, does not have a social worker making home visits from time to time, and has custody of her (his) children. The parent who has forfeited custody of her (his) children and attends Parents Anonymous for both self-help and help by the group becomes resentful of the parent who has not been "caught" and therefore does not have a social worker making home visits, or is not assigned to a probation officer, and does not have children in foster care. There is a tendency in such situations for the parent whose children are in foster care to "rat" on the parent whose children are not. In instance after instance subsequent to one parent's relinquishment of anonymity there ensued the invasion of another parent's privacy by the social worker of the no-longer anonymous parent. The tension and resulting trauma caused by the parent who did not have custody of her (his) children was dysfunctional to the point of totally disrupting the group process. In most instances the parent who had lost custody of her (his) children was negatively received by the group and in many instances was punished by ostracism. In some cases ostracism was the punishment for relinquishment of anonymity as well.

Parents Anonymous is an effective program and a viable preventive mechanism for abusive parents whose children are in their custody; but its viability is diluted and it is less of a preventive mechanism for parents whose children are in foster placement. It is next to impossible to convince a social worker, a policeman, a probation officer, or a judge handling a family case in court that there has been measureable progress in a family which is involved in Parents Anonymous and whose children are in foster placement simply because it has not been measured. Without record keeping and traditionally documented interviews, there are simply no data to indicate measureable progress. The responsibility for measuring the progress of a group member during interactions with social workers or the court system is squarely on the shoulders of the professional sponsor in the group. Unfortunately, what the profressional has for data are verbal and physical interactions with the parent at weekly meetings, home visits, and social interactions. This is viewed as "touchy-feely" data, all of which do not hold much weight in the court room when stacked against the documentation available, utilized, and offered to the court by the social worker.

Parents Anonymous is simultaneously very much like a warm family circle and a street gang. Within the circle you are surrounded by its warmth, its positive reception of you, its unconditional positive regard for you, and its ability to make sacrifices for you. But if you veer away from that circle, break it, or disrupt its form in any way, there are severe punishments. It is my observation that relinquishment of anonymity is seen by group members as breaking the circle and disrupting its form and is punishable by ostracism from the group.

This strong sanction with regard to identity concealment is not something the group members have fostered by themselves. It is fostered by the founder of the organization, Jolly K., which is a pseudonym. Many Parents Anonymous members submit poetry and stories about their everyday lives to state and national newsletters, and usually the parents give their first names only. And parents who participate in conferences, workshops, and lecture series use pseudonyms and/or modify their physical appearance by wigs or clothing unassociated with their natural personalities. This identity concealment admittedly comes from fear of exposure, but it also inspires fear of abusing parents in nonabusing parents. Thus identity concealment of members in Parents Anonymous further perpetuates the stigma associated with child abusers.

Anonymity in membership in Parents Anonymous is somewhat like the mask of the Lone Ranger who was seen as a helpful person, someone to be counted on to magically appear in a crisis; but you never knew who he was or anything else about him. Similarly, in Parents Anonymous parents know each other, communicate with each other, and help each other, but in many ways their communication is filtered through their Parents Anonymous masks. When they begin to develop outside friendships, they experience difficulty in interlocking that circle with the circle of Parents Anonymous.

Again, like street gangs, Parents Anonymous functions for the group. Thus when a member in either group begins to establish self-identity apart from the group, the group becomes threatened. The response by other members takes many forms. One form might be to make that member more powerful and place more responsibility for the group's process on her (him). Another response might be to cease supporting the member even though she (he) may still be growing and in need of group support. I observed that as soon as a group member begins to pull away or show signs of independence, the other members of the group strengthen the bonds among themselves in order to be able to deal with the independence expressed by the "maverick." If a group member chooses a course of independence, her (his) strength will be tested, as in a gang, and this strength relative to that of the group will being either the reward of leadership or the penalty of ostracism.

4 THE MORAL CAREER OF A CHILD ABUSER

In this chapter we will explore a number of concepts that we find particularly useful in addressing the changes individuals experience in self-image, skill development, and social functioning. The first of these is Goffman's concept of moral career, which involves "the regular sequence of changes...in the person's self and her (or his) framework of imagery, for judging herself (or himself) and others which she (or he) shares with others by virtue of common membership in a social category" (1961: 128). This concept is useful in exploring the relationship between response to either a group or social-category stimulus and change in self-image over time; this will be developed more fully as we present the stages in the moral career of a child abuser.

As we have said before, the child-abuse literature is replete with details of what child abusers *do* to their children. In its attempt to define the phenomenon, it describes abusive experiences and incidents. The incident is basically seen through the eyes of the victim and not the practitioner. In ascertaining and juxtaposing the practitioner's definition of abusive experiences and the literature's definition of abuse, we feel we have been able to illustrate a significant incongruence between the two. In short, previous research has told us *what* these people do but not *how* or *what* they feel about their activities. Describing the wounds on a child's body is an unreliable way to understand how and what a parent, the practitioner, was feeling before, during, and after an abusive incident.

These feelings are of extreme significance, for it is specifically these feelings that affect one's decision to seek out and affiliate with Parents Anonymous. How this period of affiliation affects feelings about past behavior, which contributes to the shaping of the novel conduct, and how the novel conduct matures into a career of conduct, is the subject matter for this chapter. And since there is insufficient previous research clarifying the relationship that self-perception and performance share with respect to child abusers as practitioners of deviant childrearing patterns, we are hopeful that the insights provided herein will serve as inducements for future researchers interested in empirical investigations of the symbiotic relationship shared by self-help group therapy and the forming of a moral career.

In addition to Goffman's concepts, we find Matza's (1969) concepts of affiliation and neutralization useful for our purposes. Affiliation describes the process by which an individual converts to conduct that is novel for him (or her) but already established for others. By providing new meaning for conduct previously regarded as outlandish or inappropriate, affiliation provides the context and process by which the neophyte may be "turned on" or "out."

The decision to affiliate is a useful one for the individual involved; while it offers him or her a way to recognize his or her conduct as nonideal or discrediting, the recognition is neutralized. It is this concept and period of neutralization which serve to enhance self-image and social functioning, the latter because of the individual's newly discovered freedom to reject the stigma which accompanies discrediting conduct or discrediting information.

Stigma as used by Goffman (1963: 3) refers to "the situation of the individual who is disqualified from full social acceptance," or "an attribute that is deeply discrediting." Being a child abuser is consistent with both of those conditions. What should be established here is that *stigma* is a situational issue which emerges not of itself but rather in a context of relationships. Discussing how you physically assaulted your child is deviant and would stigmatize you in a certain context—such as over the stuffed mushrooms at a cocktail party—but not at a Parents Anonymous meeting.

In the context of a Parents Anonymous meeting the individual does not have to be concerned with whether the external audience is aware of the "deviance," nor must the individual be concerned with "passing" or concealment. In the moral career of a child abuser, issues of "passing" come long after the learning of the stigma or of the process of becoming someone who is stigmatized or disqualified from full social acceptance due to discrediting information.

Although Goffman does not use child abusers for examples in his theoretical designs, the examples he uses have relevance to the child abusers contemplating their "stigma" in our study. Like a handicapped person, the child abuser is usually unaware that he or she is different until he or she enters into a situation where the realization becomes unavoidable. For child abusers who seek out Parents Anonymous, such realization may be voluntary or involuntary. By this we mean that individuals may seek out threatening situations *to see how* different they are, or they may be forced into threatening situations (e.g., by law enforcers or social workers) to be *shown* how different they are. In any case, it is at this point that the moral career of a child abuser begins.

Since the publication of *Social Pathology,* (Lemert: 1951), many sociologists have become interested in approaching the study of deviance by deemphasizing the causal question and emphasizing the process of response to deviance. We, like Lemert, are also concerned with the practitioners' (deviants') definitions of their activities and their definitions of themselves, and we feel that the concepts of moral career and neutralization are particularly useful in pointing to a relationship between the processes of response to deviance and the definition of conduct and self.

To some, the term "moral career" may seem subjective, with some judgmental connotations, but this is not the case at all. A dictionary definition of career is "progress or general course of action of a person through...some profession or undertaking, some moral or intellectual action...." The concept of moral career—and our own study—implies neither success nor failure, but rather a natural history of experience. That a child abuser in Parents Anonymous has a moral career is evident to us, and we feel that we can demonstrate this by presenting and illustrating the various stages or phases that a child abuser passes through before discrediting information is transformed into positive data.

Goffman deals with two phases of the mental patient's moral career: (1) the period prior to entering the hospital, which he calls the prepatient phase, and (2) the period in the hospital, or the inpatient phase; the expatient phase is not dealt with. In looking at the moral career of a child abuser we will be dealing with the three major phases: (1) the period prior to joining Parents Anonymous, which we will call the pre-acknowledgment phase, (2) the period of Parents Anonymous membership, self-acknowledgment, and (3) the period of graduation from Parents Anonymous, or becoming an ex-abuser.

On the basis of extensive observation, the moral career of a child abuser who joins Parents Anonymous appears to have six stages:

1. Being different and feeling guilty

2. Moral identification

3. Apprenticeship and moral frustration

4. Becoming a self-acknowledged child abuser

5. Being different and feeling competent

6. Moral self-acceptance and becoming a recuiter

In the rest of this discussion we will elaborate on these stages.

While what we have outlined describes the complete moral career for child abusers who affiliate with Parents Anonymous, we would not want to mislead our readers into thinking that all child abusers, even those in Parents Anonymous, go through all the stages. For example, some people never experience "being different and feeling competent," and it is these people who remain in need of the constant support and reinforcement unique to self-help therapy; however, they appear to be a minority. The outstanding feature of this self-help approach is that the majority of its participants experience complete careers, become "moral" graduates, and preserve the organization by staying with the program as ex-abusers who identify and recruit people into the pre-acknowledgment phase.

How long each phase takes to complete itself may vary with the individual; some stages may repeat themselves. For instance, in many cases stages 1 to 3 are repeated many times before transition into stage 4 is completed. This is due chiefly to the anxiety created within individuals when they start wanting to "come out" of their closeted world and admit, mainly to themselves, to being child abusers. Length of stages may also vary with the structure of each Parents Anonymous group. And before we elaborate on the stages in the moral career, this issue of group structure deserves some cursory consideration.

Each of these Parents Anonymous groups has a chairperson who is a parent member, and a professional sponsor who is not a member of the group (i.e., the sponsor is not seeking help from the group for a problem related to child abuse) but is there to offer guidance and support to the individual members, the group as a whole, and the chairperson. While there is no selection of *members* according to special or technical competence, a sponsor is selected by the group members on the basis of special competence in areas of interpersonal relationships. The role of this sponsor and his or her influence on the group appears to be a significant one. Where a group has a strong, aggressive sponsor who is capable of creating and sustaining inter-personal relationships and who can foster and reconcile models of consensus as well as conflict among the group members, then that group's members will experience a "completed career" sooner, and the repeating of internal cycles within the career will be minimal.

Parenthetically we would like to say that the sponsor's role in a Parents Anonymous group is analogous to the role that training wheels play on a child's first "two-wheeler." With the help and sup-port of a good set of training wheels, it is possible for a child to lose and regain balance time and time again while learning how to ride a bicycle. Thus, with the help and support of a good sponsor, it is possible for a child abuser to lose and regain balance while learning how to become an ex-abuser. Just as the neophyte bicycle rider depends on the training wheels *at the beginning* for balance, so the member in the pre-acknowledgment phase depends on a group's spon-sor for balance during the first three stages in his or her career.

Also, and again based on our extensive observations, it appears that a "completed career" is contingent on consistency and continuity of interaction by a group with the *same* sponsor. If a group throws its members into different settings with different sponsors every six months, let us say, then the first three stages are apt to repeat themselves each time, making it difficult for the individual to "learn of the stigma," as Goffman tells us, and to acknowledge being a child abuser. Keeping these observations in mind, we will be able to under-stand better the following stages.

STAGE 1:   BEING DIFFERENT AND FEELING GUILTY

In *Notes on the Management of Spoiled Identity,* Goffman says:

> Persons who have a particular stigma tend to have similar learning experiences regarding their plight, and similar changes in conception of self—a similar "moral career" that is both cause and effect of commitment to a similar sequence of personal adjustments. (1963: 32)

That these individuals have similar learning experiences is not to say that the experiences are uncomplicated. To the contrary, the men and women who come to identify themselves as "being different" ex-perience a complex process. Just as the first phase in the moral career of Goffman's mental patient is to a feeling about "being different," so we find the "pre-acknowledged" abuser identifying with feelings of "being different." It is this recognition of "being different" that puts the individual on a course of rejecting his or her old self-image, thereby transforming discrediting information into positive, acceptable data. Writing about the moral career of a mental patient, Goffman tells us:

> Presumably these recruits have found themselves acting *in a way* which is evidence to them that they are losing their minds or losing control of themselves....Coupled with the person's disintegrative re-evaluation...will be the new, almost equally pervasive circumstance of attempting to conceal from others...the new fundamental facts ...and attempting to discover whether others, too, have discovered them. (1961: 131-133)

Although the child abusers in our sample were not mental patients, some did feel as if they were losing their minds and others felt they were disintegrating. But the common denominators shared by these child abusers were that initial feeling of "being different" and the guilt which accompanied their disintegrated re-evaluation. They felt that not being quite like other people was somehow their fault and thus felt guilty about being different.

Question: Could you tell me where you were and what you were doing when you first suspected you were a child abuser?

Response: Well, I was a young child when I first suspected that I was, well, different. When I first hit my boy—I knew, right then. But I was so scared that I just didn't know what to do....I would hit them, feel guilty, then I would feel very much relieved and stop, but I never really tried to really stop it. Well, I could never tell my mother, but she suspected—she could see the marks and stuff but she would never say anything. But I would never talk to her. With my husband, he would see me do it but we would never sit down and talk about it.

Question: Did you talk to anybody about it?

Response: No I didn't trust anybody enough for them to understand.

Question: What do you think someone's response would have been had you talked to them about it?

Response: They really would have condemned me for it. I would have been made to feel much worse than I did at the time. And I knew my mother would have made me feel this way. (Interview #2)

Response: Where was I? I was in the bedroom having a tantrum with the children. Every day I had been yelling and one of them was doing something that I absolutely couldn't stand. I was beating on the four of them. I wasn't even letting them escape out of the room. I was hitting and kicking and smashing and trying to find something to hit them all with. I had lost total control. I felt that I was pretty rotten and pretty bad. I knew what I was doing to the children. I hated myself. (Interview #4)

Response: I was at home, and I had just completely lost control. I had spanked my son to a point where I just threw him on the bed. He had done something very minor. I had been feeling really sorry for myself for like two or three weeks before this all happened. I was depressed, I was crying, I was alone. I had some personal problems with a boyfriend, splitting up, and I was all by myself. And the kids were just...they weren't being obnoxious or anything, they were just being boys. They did something that upset me. I can't remember what it was, but it was very minor at the time. I took him to the bedroom and I spanked him and spanked him and spanked him. I threw him on the bed and I walked out. I went into my room and laid down and I cried and cried. I thought, There's something wrong with me. This just isn't normal. There's something wrong. I have a problem. I thought I was going crazy. I really did. I thought, There's something wrong with me. I had seen over television, call this number, and I thought, I am calling. I can't stand it any more. I called and I told the lady, "There's something wrong with me. I've lost control. I can't stand this anymore. I'm going nuts." (Interview #9)

Response: I had always thought that I was doing something wrong, but I didn't know what. I know that the things I was doing with my child were things that I felt guilty about. I didn't know why I was doing them. (Interview #13)

Response: I think I had trouble coping from the time Peter was just a few months old. He never responded very much to me...even as a tiny baby, and I didn't expect him to right away, but after the months went on and on and I tried to hold him and talk to him, he turned away. So I moved him, and then he turned the other way...he wouldn't even look at me. And I started thinking, what's wrong with me, and that's when it started. (Interview #26)

At this point in the process, locating available information concerning support services to parents who are losing control becomes the next crucial step in the moral career of a child abuser. The parents suspect that they are different and they do something about it. What many of them do *not* do is discuss their feelings with family or a friend. In most cases there are no friends or family available, or those who would be available are too threatening to the "different" individual who fears their subjective judgments and condemnations.

Question: When you first suspected that you were a child abuser, with whom did you talk?

Response: I wasn't...getting along with my mother at the time...there were no relatives. My brother was never around....There was no one.

Question: How did that affect you?

Response: It made me feel worse. As a parent I felt like a failure. I couldn't even talk to anybody about this problem. Because I knew what they would say. (Interview #2)

This initial time of "being different and feeling guilty" coupled with the agony of remaining relatively invisible to the public and to whatever family and friends exist is particularly stressful. These people feel "strange," "different," "out of it," and "guilty," and yet they must maintain something of a facade for onlookers until they can grasp a term, a name, or a feeling they can relate to or identify with.

Some may seek out professionals to help them find a name for this feeling with which they are struggling. In many cases these individuals seek out family physicians as sounding boards for their feelings, to no avail. Some enter into relationships with professional counselors while others join a "Dreikurs group." There are even those who temporarily accept such labels as "psychotic," "nervous," "frigid," "impotent," "juvenile," "selfish," "neurotic," or just plain "mean."

Question: Could you identify *how* or *what* you felt when you were abusing your child?

Response: I don't know....I think there was some other reason why [I was abusive]. It could've been just myself I wanted to punish....I don't know, for some reason my therapist diagnosed me as a masochist. (Interview #13)

These attempts at tentative identifications quickly fail to provide the individual with the appropriate term which could express or make a connection with *how* he or she feels. These people may temporarily respond to a variety of labels or names, and they may undergo periods of tentative identifications, but until they can connect *how* they feel with an appropriate term, we merely have attempts at self-conception.

The duration of this period of "being different and feeling guilty" and of attempting to try tentative identifications is different for each child abuser. But the moment must come when, either through interactions with counselors, casual conversations, or independently, they identify with a name or a term and attempt to "try on for size" the label of child abuser.

Before they become aware of the name of this thing that makes them feel different or guilty, they are quite aware of what is "normative."

Question: Could you tell me how you used to feel about people who are child abusers?

Response: When my children were very little and I didn't really feel I had a problem, at that time, until they got a little bit older, if I had read newspaper articles about something like this, it really frightened me to think that there would be people like this. At the same time it made me really feel sorry. Not so much for the child but also for the parent that had done that thing. I thought after reading articles or newspaper clippings, things like this, that the parent must have really needed help. (Interview #10)

Response: I always thought it was terrible. I remember that they used to play up things in the paper when something awful happened. They never put in articles about child abuse that happened casually. It was always parents who killed their child or really beat them up. But then thinking about it in terms of myself—before I read the article about Parents Anonymous—I never thought of my behavior as child abuse. (Interview #11)

Response: I thought it was the most repulsive thing and I couldn't understand how people could do that. To me it was inhuman. I could not understand, especially reading in the paper how someone could kill their child, or beat him. And a lot of other things....Well, I never realized the pattern that went on. And the cycle that went on. That I was repeating what my parents had done. In church one day, I wanted to put my head on Mom's shoulder. She just shrugged me away from her. No affection shown. None whatsoever. She never showed any affection to my father, and she never showed any to my brother. I found myself being the same way with my son. It's very hard for me to show any kind of affection. (Interview #13)

STAGE 2: MORAL IDENTIFICATION

Precisely at the moment when a person can connect his or her feelings with the appropriate term depicting those feelings—in this case the term "child abuser"—it can be said that he or she has moved into the second stage of Phase 1 in their moral career, the stage of moral identification.

For many, moral identification takes place independently; possibly they were reading an article about child abusers and they identified with the protagonist, or perhaps they were impressed by a news story about a family with a child-abuse problem, and they found that they could relate to the family's problems. For others, the moment of moral identification comes as a result of some social interaction where, with friends or family, it is conveyed to them that their behavioral patterns are not "normative." We submit that while the Phase 1 pre-acknowledged abuser is aware of his or her "differentness," he or she is also aware of what the "normative" pattern is. Being aware of both patterns does not necessarily imply skill in both patterns of behavior; while the individual may know how to be different, he or she may not know how to be normative.

At this point in the child abuser's moral career it is unimportant for him or her to talk about "normative" patterns. It is much more important to be able to talk about "different" patterns, and how he or she feels "different." And it is at the moment when the term *child abuser* appropriately names people's feelings and behavior that they enter into the stage of moral identification with that name.

Question: How did you first hear about Parents Anorymous?

Response: I first read about Parents Anonymous in a magazine. As soon as I read about it, I had the feeling that I should go to meetings like this. I would be in touch with other people that have angry feelings towards their children and took them out on their children. I tried to find out if there was a chapter like this in my area. (Interview #10)

Response: There was an article in one of the daily newspapers. I think I called immediately after reading it. Then I think I called this other friend of mine to tell her....It was about parents who had problems with child abuse and it said that they could get help from this particular group....I thought it was great. (Interview #11)

Question: What did you think about the organization when the counselor told you about it? You said...you identified with it...you thought it would be good for you.

Response: He didn't say it was for child abusers. And then it dawned on me what this meeting was. You don't have to be a real killer to go there, you just got to think maybe you could. I did give my Eric a little black eye, and then I gave Markie one yesterday....I was trying to hit him with the stick, and he went upstairs and hid under the sleeping bag, and I was hitting him on...which I thought was the butt, and then he comes out of the blanket. I looked at his eye, and I really felt bad...[you] think of things more when you're going there. I would have thought it was nothing. I'd say, "Gee, look what I did, I'm sorry kid," but now when I go there, I'm thinking, oh, a black eye on a kid...you know, [it] makes you think more of what else could come next. If I didn't stop banging on him he might have had two of them. (Interview #27)

Earlier we made the statement that while an individual may "know" about both "normative" and "different" patterns of behavior, he or she may not possess skills in both areas. While an individual may know full well when he or she is losing control or when he or she is out of control, that same individual may not know how to manage that behavior. It appears that this inadequate or inappropriate behavioral management serves as a constant reinforcement of the individual's "differentness." As these parents learn from Parents Anonymous to manage the "different" behavior, their moral identification with the name child abuser strengthens. As their identification strengthens, so does their desire to learn about the category with which they identify. What they know is *how* to be different; what they want to learn is how to become "not different."

STAGE 3:   APPRENTICESHIP AND MORAL FRUSTRATION

Once individuals have expressed an identification with the term child abuser and have done so by regularly attending the Parents Anonymous meetings for a period of time, they are then ready to learn how they are "different" and how to become "not different." The duration of this period between moral identification and apprenticeship may vary from group to group; this variance is due largely to the strength or lack of strength possessed both by the chapter chairperson and the chapter sponsor. Where the sponsor supports and reinforces the chairperson, the period between moral identification and apprenticeship will be abbreviated for the members in that group. Again, based on our extensive observations, if the chapter sponsor quietly waits for a behavioral change to materialize in the participants without engaging them in exercises where they can experience change as a reaction to stimulus from a group, an individual, or themselves, it will take a much longer time to pass from moral identification to apprenticeship, and feelings of self-doubt will be more prevalent.

Some of the previously mentioned research in juvenile delinquency draws a correlation between delinquent behavior and lack of a model for the young person to emulate or imitate. In Parents Anonymous the sponsor and often the chairperson serve as models for the member. We found the characteristics of sponsor-chairperson models to be a combination of self-confidence and aggressiveness, with particular emphasis on competence in handling interpersonal relationships; thus they make good teachers for the apprentices.

One of the first things taught to an apprentice is the concept of an "alternative" to abusive behavior. Although Parents Anonymous claims that an "alternative" is simply another and a more comfortable way of doing something, its real accomplishment is exposing the apprentice to a normative pattern of response to stimulus. The stimulus comes particularly from a child in their care but may also come from groups and other individuals. The apprentice learns how to manage his or her behavior in social interactions; with the support and reinforcement of the chapter chairperson and sponsor, the apprentice learns skills in effective "behavior management."

Question: In reading some of the Parents Anonymous literature, I have run across the word "alternative." Could you tell me what an alternative is?

Response: In the beginning it was mostly about childproofing my apartment and putting gates on doors, and most of the stress I was under simply was because I didn't know how to deal with a small child. He was getting into everything and driving me crazy. And provoking me in a hundred different ways. It never occurred to me to move all the cleaning solutions and cleansers to a higher shelf so he couldn't get into them.

Question: Had you considered these alternatives?

Response: I never thought of them. I was told to put the cleansers from under the sink on a high shelf. You block off the doorway. He would pull everything from the drawers in his room. There was no door in his room. I was told to block off that room somehow so he couldn't get in there. I was told exactly what to do and I needed that

Question: Can you be more specific about how Parents Anonymous helps?

Response: Parents Anonymous gives you something to do besides abusing. It gives you alternatives; instead of hitting, instead of name calling, it gives you something to do. Instead of throwing a child, you throw a cup or a plate. Instead of responding to a temper tantrum with a temper tantrum of your own, you lock yourself in a bedroom until it's over. Something to do instead of abusing.

Question: So an alternative is something you use instead of abusing?

Response: Right.

Question: Could you give me a specific example or an incident where you use "alternatives"?

Response: Yeah, there's one that stands out in my mind because it scared me a whole lot at the time. I forget what the situation was, but I was very upset and very angry at my son, and I was going to pick him up and do God knows what with him. But he was standing next to a little plastic coaster wagon. I went for him and at the last minute I grabbed the wagon and I smashed it against the wall. It smashed into a dozen different pieces. That's how furious I was. If that had been my son, he probably would have been dead.

Question: Where or from whom did you first hear about alternatives?

Response: From Parents Anonymous. (Interview #1)

Question: Could you tell me what an "alternative" is?

Response: We'll use the telephone thing. That's an alternative. Instead of beating your kid, you get to the phone....You go to the phone and you break the thought of hitting your child. You are using that phone at that instant. It changes your pattern. It's an alternative

Question: Where did you first hear about "alternatives"?

Response: Through Parents Anonymous. (Interview #6)

Question: Do other members in your group use "alternatives"?

Response: Yeah.

Question: How do you know?

Response: Well, we talk about them. We try and set goals for ourselves. A new member that we have feels guilty, she doesn't work, she doesn't get up and fix breakfast for her children. They are old enough to make breakfast for themselves, but she feels guilty about this. So she's attempting to get up, wake up, get them breakfast. (Interview #26)

This period of apprenticeship is the most difficult stage in Phase 1 and requires the most time to complete. The apprentice while in this stage must make attempts to perform "normatively" and must also experience a fair amount of success. Since the number of failures will be greater than the number of successes, the apprentice often experiences moral frustration.

This moral frustration not only comes when the individual has failed, but also when he or she attempts to perform "normatively" and succeeds. As Goffman points out, the friendships and acquaintances made subsequent to a stigmatizing experience may be easier to maintain than those made prior to the stigmatizing event. Prior to entering the stage of apprenticeship, the individuals had established a pattern of behaving, and were accepted, tolerated, or rejected on the basis of that behavior by whatever family or friends they had. Now that they are apprentices they have two camps of people to deal with: the "old friends" who remember them only the way they were and the "new friends" in Parents Anonymous who support and reinforce their attempts to *become different* from the way they were.

On the one hand, the frustration comes to the fore when, in attempting to perform normatively, Parents Anonymous members who are trying to change their behavior threaten and/or instill insecurities in the first group or are "put down" by persons in the first group who say things such as "you can't teach an old dog new tricks," "you'll always be the same," "people never change," or, and the most damaging, "it's in your blood and ain't nothin' you can do about it." On the other hand, the frustration materializes when they fail in their attempt to perform normatively and in failing, revert back to their "different" abusive behavior patterns. Then as apprentices they return to the group to share their failure, for which they are not rewarded, but are still given the attention, support, and reinforcement which they feel they do not deserve.

Question: Do you envision any problems created for you by your experience as a member of Parents Anonymous?

Response: There were problems in the beginning. He [husband] wouldn't accept the fact that I was a child abuser. He almost didn't like the fact that I wasn't being physical any more. He didn't mind when I didn't yell—he kind of enjoyed that. When my attitudes and behavior started to change, it was like he was trying to do things to get me back into what I was doing before. It was almost like what the children were doing. Trying to create a situation for me and at the beginning I found that very difficult to cope with. But I did have the support of that kind from four other women...I could call someone else and talk to them...I finally got to the point where I didn't care at all what my husband thought. What I was doing was strictly for myself. I almost had to throw him by the wayside in order to pick up the pieces of my own life, and he would have to fit into whatever life I formed for myself from that point on. (Interview #4)

Response: My husband didn't feel that I belonged there...he didn't stop me...he wasn't behind me 100%. (Interview #6)

Response: Yeah, at first my husband didn't really want me to be affiliated with this group. He felt that I didn't need this because I had seen a psychiatrist. He didn't feel I could be termed child-abuser. However, later on he realized how much it had helped me so he felt that it was very good for me. (Interview #10)

The moral frustration appears to diminish as success in self-management increases. As this happens, the individuals we referred to earlier as the second group—the "new friends"—become more of a dominant force in the *coming-out* process, i.e., the identification with these individuals is so great it facilitates the process by virtue of their sharing a similar social category. As members muster the courage to acknowledge and accept their problem—to actually come out in public places and say "Yes, I am a child abuser"—they simultaneously must reject the importance of the persons in their lives who knew them the way they were. They concentrate instead on the persons who know them the way they are and who support them in their attempts to learn self-management skill.

STAGE 4:   BECOMING A SELF-ACKNOWLEDGED CHILD ABUSER

As Becker (1963) points out, in order for a person to become involved in a social role, he or she must develop functionally integrated
relations with at least two people, who then form parts of his or her
social circle. Before an individual can pass from being an apprentice
to becoming a self-acknowledged child abuser, that social circle must
function to the extent that the individual learns the technique of *coming out* as a child abuser, learns to perceive the effects of his or her actions in coming out, and learns to enjoy the coming-out experience.

In learning and accepting first the notion of being different and
then the new name or label of child abuser, there appears to be a
reorganization of the individual's "story." As Goffman points out:

> in reviewing his (her) own moral career, the stigmatized in-
> dividual may single out...experiences which serve...to account
> for his (her) coming to the beliefs and practices that he (she)
> now has regarding his (her) own kind....(1963: 38-9)

Question: Could you describe an incident or experience in
which you considered yourself abusive to your child?

Response: Apparently I guess I couldn't sleep at night, I was
mad at someone. I went and got my son, and I got him up out of bed
and made him stand in the middle of the living room floor...just stand
there...he'd stand and cry, and asked if he could go back to bed, and I
said, "No, you stand there for as long as I want you to." And he kept
saying, "Please, Mommy, let me go back to bed," and I said, "No,
you're going to stand there." He just cried. It was like there was
something in the back of my head telling me "Don't do this to him."
Yet the more he kept on crying, the more I did it. (Interview #15)

Response: Well, in my good, in my good moments I can see,
I'm an adult, I know better. I should have self-control and all of this
stuff that comes with maturity. The child had done nothing. And yet
in my worst moments, I can say if the kid is so tired, why doesn't he go
to sleep. I lose all that rationality after somebody cries for over two
hours and there is nothing that you can do to make him go to sleep. I
end up throwing him into bed. I don't do that now. (Interview #21)

Before coming out, the individual must learn how to present his
or her biography to the public. The public in this case might be a radio
or television audience, a Parent-Teacher group, or an acquaintance at

a supermarket who *saw* the individual on television or *heard* him or her at the Parent Teacher meeting. These are the difficult times of coming out for the child abuser, and it is at this point that the social circle is an invaluable instrument of moral reinforcement for the neophyte who is attempting to break into normalcy and out of differentness. Usually the coming-out technique is learned from either the chairperson or sponsor or from another group member who has attempted coming out with success.

For the individual becoming a self-acknowledged child abuser, part of the process of exposure is perceiving what effects self-exposure has. The individual is reminded that his or her coming out serves as a reinforcement and as an inducement for people who feel "different" but haven't yet connected their feelings with the term child abuser. They are to recruit and identify new members by proselytizing, much in the same way that religious affiliates seek out converts. So we find that part of the process of becoming a self-acknowledged child abuser includes developing skills in identifying potential recruits, and spreading the word about Parents Anonymous by sharing their unique biographies with anyone and everyone. Although coming out is not forced, it is strongly encouraged.

Question: Are you involved in speaking to local groups about Parents Anonymous?

Response: Yes.

Question: What kinds of groups are these?

Response: Well, I've spoken with Parent-Teacher Association groups. Recently we attended a Foster Parents group. In January we have...we're planning on meeting with the Parents Without Partners group, and also with church groups.

Question: When you do speak to these local groups, what do you speak about?

Response: We talk about the fact that everyone is a potential abuser. And we get into small, intimate groups, so that usually there are three or four chapter members that go out...in these groups, and we try to split up the whole group to get into an intimate conversation with people we want to reach. (Interview #23)

Question: What kinds of things did you talk about?

Response: In my English class, I mainly wanted to get across to people that everybody can be a child abuser. It's not just a certain people picked out, and I wanted to get across the ways of child abuse, and not just physical, because there are other ways. And if they ever knew of any case, or suspected, to call someone, so that that person could get help. (Interview #19)

As the individual becomes more involved in coming out, much enjoyment is derived, and another reshaping of the biography takes place.

STAGE 5: BEING DIFFERENT AND FEELING COMPETENT

During this period the individual is once again different, but there is a sense of accomplishment accompanied by a feeling of professional competence in the field of child abuse. It is at this point that the individual's self-image undergoes dramatic change. As we said before, these parents once again feel "different" from other people, but for different reasons. Now they feel, and have been convinced to feel, that they have expertise in an area and have been adequately trained to share it with others. They know something that others do not: they know what it's like to feel "different" and maybe crazy; they know what it's like to identify with the Parents Anonymous jargon; they know what it's like to be an apprentice in the program and learn how to use "alternatives" successfully; they know about the frustration of failure coupled with familial pressures not to try to change their "different" habits; they know what it feels like to come out and say openly "I am a child abuser"; and they know how to identify people who are "different." Knowing all of this and knowing that they can articulate this knowledge to persons who do not have it is a source of enjoyment for the individual who at this point enters the process of "becoming an ex-abuser."

According to Becker, the final stage of "becoming" involves the individual and the member of his or her social circle incorporating the role's behavior and its identities into his or her own personality. This applies to individuals "becoming ex-abusers" as they move into the final stage of their moral careers as child abusers.

STAGE 6: MORAL SELF-ACCEPTANCE AND BECOMING A RECRUITER

At this point the individual is no longer concerned with constructing a unit of permissible information with respect to his or her social identity. The once discrediting information is transformed into information that is creditable. It is no longer necessary to avoid discovery. The result of this process is an individual who has a keen, clear sense of identity and one who has, in his or her attempts to perform normatively, internalized the normative pattern as his or her own.

Question: How old was your child when you joined Parents Anonymous?

Response: He was five.

Question: What was it like with your child before you joined Parents Anonymous?

Response: It was pretty miserable. There was no communication. There was a lot of hollering and screaming. I can remember wanting to be alone a lot. I never felt like I had any time to myself. I would shoo Chris off to bed and that's usually when the abuse would start. He would go into bed and feel—signs of rejection. He would come back and say, "Mom, can I stay up?" And I said, "If you know what's good for you, you'll go back to bed." He would keep coming back until I would start either spanking him [or] hitting and slapping his hands. "Now will you go to bed?" And he kept coming back for more. Now I realize that was his only means of attention. The only kind of attention he got from me was when he was bad. I had nobody to say, "Here, will you keep him for an hour? Until I get my thoughts collected?" There was nobody to baby-sit for me, no time to call my own. He stayed up as late as I did, he got up when I did. There was no time for me. I don't know, it got to the point where I really resented him.

Question: Do you feel your affiliation with Parents Anonymous has changed you in any way?

Response: Yes, I do. It's made me aware of, number 1, a lot of us do the things I was doing, number 2, my Chris reacting the way he was, for attention, and number 3, the idea that if I come in crisis, that there's somebody there that can help me out of it. (Interview #13)

Question: Has your involvement with Parents Anonymous helped you in some specific ways?

Response: Yeah, all of them.

Question: How?

98

Response: It has made me think more of myself. It has made me think enough of myself to go after what I want....I've only gotten one job since I've been involved in Parents Anonymous. But I think I came across very different in the interview than I ever have in the past. And on the job now, working, I feel a lot more self-confident, I am able to stand up for myself when I am accused of things I'm not responsible for, which I've never done. Before I had never been able to do that. I am able to not feel terribly dejected and depressed over mistakes I make. This is the good difference I found when going back to work now from when I was working before. Any little mistake I made I was terrified to let anyone know about it. Of course, when you work in bookkeeping and accounting and stuff, you make a mistake, you have to fix it because it's going to turn up somewhere or another if it's not fixed, and it always did, and I was always miserable about it and felt like I was very incompetent because of it. And now, I find I've made a mistake and I don't even say, well, "I'm sorry." I don't apologize for it. I just say hey, such and such—this is what has to be done to correct it. I found that big difference there. I feel really good about knowing what to do to rectify mistakes. Which I never did before because I never tried to rectify them. I just got down on myself about them.

Question: What kind of a self-image do you have now?

Response: Oh, it's a great deal improved over what it used to be. I'm pretty okay.

Question: What kind of words might describe you now?

Response: Assertive; I assert myself. I stick up for myself now. I don't let people walk all over me. I've got some self-confidence now. If I know what I'm doing and somebody else doesn't like it and I believe in it, I'll go ahead and do it anyway and not feel bad about it. I feel a whole lot less abusive....Abusing my son was a way of abusing myself. When I stopped abusing him to some degree I started seeing all the ways I was abusing myself and I put a stop to most of them....It's made me feel that I'm worth a little bit of trouble now. (Interview #1)

Of interest here is whether or not this entire process places labeling theory in a precarious position. In studies of deviance, labeling theory suggests that

> social groups create deviance by making rules whose infraction constitutes deviance....deviance is not a quality of the act the

person commits but rather a consequence of the application by others of rules and sanctions to an "offender."...So deviance is a consequence of the responses of others to a person's act. (Becker, 1963: 9).

The offender's behavior is named and learned by others who are onlookers. Further, labeling theory suggests that the offender accepts and internalizes the label. The practitioner of deviant acts must do so in the context of onlookers, who then proceed to define the acts as "deviant." Therefore a child abuser is not a child abuser until that status or role has been conferred upon him or her through legal authority. Only then can the individual be considered labeled. What we must recognize and continue to explore in studies of deviance is the practitioner's self-definition and his or her potential to reject a label created by his or her audience incongruent with his or her own. That is to say, before we can define the act as deviant, we must compare the practitioner's definition of the act with that of the onlooker's. As a society of onlookers we are more prone to label those whose social status is at the lower end of the ladder; thus we label the illiterate and the poor as child abusers much more quickly than we would a middle-class, college-educated individual. But that doesn't negate the existence of that self-definition among middle-class, college-educated people who "feel different." It is our sincere hope that we have placed a serious dent in the position held by many that child abusing is a class-linked, age-linked, or income-linked characteristic.

Jolly K. describes herself as someone who has "made it out of abuse." She is an extraordinarily charismatic individual who builds relationships based on a belief in unconditional positive regard. And while others may see her as "kinky" or "weird," her unilateral rejection of stigma makes it difficult for the onlookers, the audience, to persevere in their belief in the discrediting information which was an embarrassment to her. She changed herself and is a source of reinforcement and inspiration for others who want to change.

Question: Have you totally rejected your past self-image?

Response: No, I've accepted it. It's a part of me. That's the way I was at one time. I'm not that way now. I'm not miserable now. I'm not a monster now, but there was a time I told myself I was. And that's the way I was. I've accepted it.

Question: Could you sum up how you've changed yourself so you no longer see yourself the way you once were?

Response: It was a long, slow process of deciding exactly what I didn't like about myself and finding out what I had to do to change what I didn't like. So that I could like myself. Changing my reactions. Changing my destructive attitude toward myself and other people... the way I thought about myself. Thinking about myself as a person who does have rights and who does deserve some of the good things. (Interview #1)

Being a child abuser, like being gay, is a stigma that carries with it a series of moral imputations with respect to character and personality. Both traits tend to strip individuals of their identities and respectabilities.

The moral career of a child abuser must remind us that as human beings we have the capacity to change, and the moral career of a child abuser is an illustration for social scientists of the potency of human life.

5 SOCIALIZATION, NEUTRALIZATION, AND "CAREERS OF AFFILIATION"

The foci of this study have been, first, the lives of individuals who, either voluntarily or involuntarily, became involved in self-help group therapy because they experienced problems while attempting to raise their children without harming them physically and/or emotionally, and, second, their eventual identification with the words *child abuser*. Another concern of the study was to determine what, if any, relationship existed between involvement in self-help group therapy and changes experienced in parent-child relationships, social functioning, and self-image. In this regard we found that, unlike the careers of most individuals defined as deviant and processed through specialized institutions, that of the child abuser runs a course toward moral acceptance or moral reinstatement. We suggest that this change in reaction and self-definition over a period of time is primarily a function of the self-help therapy group which served as an agent of adult socialization during an adult life crisis; the techniques of neutralization (Sykes and Matza, 1957) or methods of evasion and self-protection used by the participants involved in the self-help therapy groups; and the decision to affiliate with the self-help therapy group, maturing into a "career of affiliation."

The individuals who became involved with Parents Anonymous during the period of our investigation did so at a time when their lives were filled to overflowing with failure, isolation, and crisis—the period of early parenthood. Their shared problem was that they were seen by others and by themselves as ineffective, inadequate individuals who were harmful to the children in their keeping. They were child abusers. When confronted with parenthood they found it to be an ambiguous situation lacking clear definitions of behavioral expectations for both themselves and their children.

In their attempts to define this ambiguous situation and to adopt coping strategies for dealing with the crisis of isolation and failure,

101

they discovered they could neither respond nor initiate an activity characteristic of parenthood. They were neither appropriately equipped nor adequately prepared by prior life experiences, however varying, to deal with the crisis they experienced during the early years of parenthood. We believe the self-help therapy groups with which these individuals became involved acted as agents of socialization, not only because they transmitted norms, values, attitudes, and concepts with respect to parenting and adulthood, but also because they offered the individuals opportunities to experience a learning process concerned with role performance and behaviors expected by others, as well as by the individuals themselves, with respect to parenting and adulthood. These self-help therapy groups for child abusers became more than just that; for the individuals involved, they became places to learn about rules, expectations, and right and not-so-right behavior. As many respondents pointed out they became "awareness groups."

Question: Do you do anything to prevent people from finding out that you go to Parents Anonymous meetings?

Response: No, but I don't call it a crisis group, I call it a women's consciousness group.

Question: Are you saying that it raised your level of awareness to certain things?

Response: Oh yes, yes, definitely yes....I don't think I was blind, I think I just didn't see...because maybe people didn't have the time to sit down and talk to me about it.

Question: What is it you think that you are seeing now that you didn't see before?

Response: Well, I'm seeing that I'm worth something which I never saw before....I never had pride in myself and I would down him [my son] a lot and I've learned that's not correct....I've learned to leave him alone instead of downing him verbally...that's something terrible and wrong....I see that now...the group's helped me see that....(Interview #23)

As Becker points out (1963: 1) all social groups have rules, expectations, and right and wrong behavior. There are basically two ways to approach the study of persons who break the rules, fall short of the group expectations, and engage in wrong behavior: engage those people whose job it is to enforce the rules in lengthy discussions concerning the definitions and descriptions of rule-breaking situations and wrong behavior, in an effort to ascertain what it is that a particular form of deviance practiced by "outsiders" consists of; or enter into dialogue with the "deviance-practicing outsider," the rule-breaker, in an effort to define and describe the meaning of the rule-breaking behavior. We chose the second approach as the method for our study chiefly because we felt it would best enable us to tackle a problem which deserves major attention, i.e., the incongruities and incon- sistencies between the visual and intellectual illusions about the social reality of a world of child abusers and the reality that exists. By going out *to* the child abusers and staying with them we were able to observe their attempts to be nonabusive parents and to function well socially, attempts which repeatedly failed, and failed miserably. We were also privy to their unguarded explanations for their failure, which basically had to do with the absence of a learning process that would have ade- quately, appropriately, and effectively prepared them for the adult life crisis of parenting.

Question: Could you recall when you first suspected that you had a problem with child abuse?

Response: I think it was when we had our first child. I wasn't used to...to babies, kids hollering...I just wasn't used to it, I coulán't shut him up and that made me more nervous and we ran into problems of we couldn't go out when we wanted to because we had the baby and we had to find a sitter right after he was born. (Interview #31)

Question: Before you became a mother, what were your expec- tations of being a mother? What was it going to be like?

Response: It was going to be having a little girl...who was always dressed up, and who I would take everyplace with me...and just love...but it wasn't like I thought it would be...we stayed home...and I wanted to go out...explaining to people about having an illegitimate child...worried about the stigma....(Interview #8)

This learning process to which we referred earlier can be defined as a socialization process through which norms, values, attitudes, beliefs, customs and concepts are transmitted from one generation to the next. It is helpful to understand this process of social learning, as it closely parallels the learning process experienced by the individuals in our study who were members of the Parents Anonymous groups we observed. For our purposes, the socialization process can be defined as consisting of the transmission, internalization, and retransmission of these norms and values, et al. for recruitment.

The first of the three stages in the process of socialization involves the transmission of group values, norms, and behavioral expectations and techniques by either direct or indirect methods. Two sets of individuals are involved: the individual transmitting the norms, etc., and the individuals to whom the transmission is directed.

Generally, the first group any individual becomes a member of is his or her family, within which are varietal norms, values, and behavioral expectations and techniques which are transmitted either directly or indirectly. In most cases the transmission is carried out by a member, or members, of senior standing in that group. In the case of the family the transmitting members would include the parents, older siblings, and/or extended-family relations who would accomplish transmission either verbally or nonverbally. For instance, techniques which could be transmitted both through verbal instruction and non-verbal communication, i.e., through observation of the example of others who eat with their elbows off the dinner table.

Although our example is admittedly a simple one, the process of transmission that we are discussing closely parallels that observed by LeMasters (1975), whose data revealed that the "blue-collar aristocrats" in his study attempted to preserve their way of life by transmitting it to their sons—teaching them to define themselves physically, to be inner-directed, to "handle" women, to work with their hands, and to avoid being "a sucker." And Barbara S. Heyl in her discussion of the training of house prostitutes described in detail how techniques and attitudes for the act of fellatio are taught or transmitted to a new "turn-out" by the Madam (1975: 212-15). There are numerous studies whose findings support the idea of the transmission stage as the beginning of a social learning cycle (Becker: 1963; Davis: 1961; Rains: 1969; Sutherland: 1970).

Transmitting expectations and techniques of behavior to an individual and getting that individual to behave as expected and instructed are not easy, but may be accomplished, for example, by threatening, bribing, or even brain-washing. There is still another way, and this involves the internalization of the transmitted norms, etc., by the individual. It is during this second stage of the process of socialization, the stage of internalization, that the neophyte member, to whom the transmission process has been directed, develops into a cooperative member—cooperative not only because the norms and values have been learned, but also because they have been accepted as his or her own. Accompanying this internalization is the identification with the group and a sense of belonging based on the common feeling that their destinies are bound together by virtue of the norms, values, etc., which they share. Only as the neophyte member identifies with the group and emotionally accepts the moral validity of these shared norms can it be said that he or she is a cooperative member.

"The crucial characteristic of cooperation...is the mutual advantageousness of the relationship" (Lundberg, 1954: 441). That the members develop an identification with the group and express a mutual agreement with respect to norms are important not only for the maintenance of the group, but also for its preservation and continuation, the latter depending mainly on the recruitment of new members. This is the final stage in the process of socialization as earlier defined and is carried out by those members who are "cooperative" and who become "active members" the moment they engage in recruitment. When the neophyte member becomes a recruiting member, thereby achieving active-member status within the group, the cyclical socialization process has been completed.

Although we are inclined to agree with Goffman, who describes the socialization process as a "continuous process of learning to abandon old roles and self-conceptions and to acquire new ones" (1962: 482), the sequential models (Becker: 1963; Cressey: 1953; Davis: 1961; Feinbloom: 1975; Heyl: 1975; Light: 1975; Matza: 1969; Rains: 1969; Sutherland: 1970; Sykes and Matza: 1957) are more closely aligned with the process of social learning experienced by the child abusers in our study where we observed them involved in their self-help therapy groups initially as "neophyte members," then as "cooperative members," and eventually as "active members." The moral career of a child abuser and the social learning process have symbiotic relationship. In Table 14 we have outlined the sequential changes in self-definition experienced by the group member during the social learning process and the relationship of these changes to the accompanying and corresponding membership status transition of the member within the group.

With regard to explaining the changes in response and self-definition over a period of time as experienced by the individuals in our investigation, Goffman's concept of moral career and the social learning process are particularly useful. In exploring further relationship between response and self-image over time we find that "techniques of neutralization" as advanced by Sykes and Matza (1957) and affiliation as explained by Matza (1969) are helpful.

Sykes and Matza contend that their "techniques of neutralization" are actually types of definitions that are learned by juvenile delinquents as favorable to the violation of the law. These learned definitions are congruent with the delinquent behavior, and because

Table 14

Relationships: (A) Phases in the Moral Career of a Child Abuser; (B) Stages in the Moral Career of a Child Abuser; (C) Membership Status Transition within the Group; (D) Stages in the Social Learning Process

A	B	C	D
I pre-acknowledgement	1. being different and feeling guilty	neophyte	transmission
	2. Moral identification	neophyte	
	3. apprenticeship and moral frustration	cooperative	
II becoming an acknowledged abuser	4. becoming a self-acknowledged child abuser	cooperative	internalization
	5. being different and feeling competent	cooperative	
III becoming an ex-abuser	6. moral self-acceptance and becoming a recruiter	active recruitment	retransmission

they allow the delinquent to "neutralize" antidelinquent definitions, they make his or her delinquencies seem right. These favorable definitions don't really define the delinquent behavior as good; rather, their function is one of excusing or justifying the delinquent act. With these definitions the indivual is armed with sufficient equipment to maintain a good self-image. In actuality, these neutralizing definitions serve to *defend* the delinquent activity. The major forms of neutralizing definitions used by juvenile delinquents include denial of responsibility, denial of injury, denial of the victim, condemnation of the condemners, and appeal to higher loyalties.

The major forms of neutralizing definitions used by the individuals in our study closely parallel those used by the delinquents to whom Sykes and Matza refer. The neutralizing definition most commonly used by the child abusers we observed and interviewed was denial of responsibility. Much of the difficulty they experienced in passing from Stage 3 to Stage 4 in their moral careers had to do with learning a deneutralizing definition, the acceptance of responsibility, for the nonideal, abusive actions directed toward their children, coupled with the acceptance of the *importance* of those nonabusive, ideal actions. The acceptance for the responsibility of one's actions is not easy, particularly if the actions are repeated failures; it is really not surprising that juvenile delinquents and child abusers avoid the emotional acceptance of the label "deviant" by neutralizing their recognized nonideal conduct and thereby *deny* responsibility for that conduct. After all, one of the best ways to deal with repeated failures is to deny you ever wanted or cared about succeeding in the first place. And implicit in the argument set forth by Sykes and Matza concerning the "techniques of neutralization" is this notion that commitment to conformity is weakened by the neutralizing definitions. We might agree that commitment to conformity is weakened by the neutralizing definitions which enable the individual to avoid the label "deviant." But we contend that over a period of time opportunities for change in response and self-definition are strengthened if the individual enters into an affiliation with persons who *encourage* the individual to face and accept his or her conduct as nonideal, but who *discourage* the emotional acceptance of himself or herself as nonideal.

> In its most human form, affiliation describes the process by which the subject is converted to conduct novel for him (or her) but already established for others...and by providing new meanings for conduct previously regarded as outlandish or inappropriate, affiliation provides the context and process by which the neophyte may be "turned on" or "out." (Matza, 1969: 101-2)

As the individual begins to face and accept his or her nonideal conduct in the context of the affiliation, the recognition of this discrediting information is cushioned, or neutralized, by the individual's participation in new or novel conduct which has already been established by others with whom the individual affiliates. In his discussion of affiliation Matza develops the idea of contagion as a natural prelude to conversion, but we suggest that it is neither the stage of contagion nor the period of conversion that has significant effect on response and self-definition over a period of time. Rather, it is the desire or willingness, coupled with the commitment to make a career of affiliation, which influences greatly the transformation of the discrediting information into positive data. We define this career of affiliation as follows: a sequence of social experiences followed by an emergence of motivational awareness influenced largely by the individual's desire to fashion, from an affiliation, an occupational category defined by the individual as his or her life's work. Further we suggest that this concept of a career of affiliation is particularly useful in exploring the relationship between response and self-definition over a period of time and in the subsequent rejection of stigma.

In the case of the individuals we observed, the occupational category which they fashioned from their affiliation with Parents Anonymous as child abusers is best described as that of an "experienced child abuser, skilled as a lay therapist." There is hardly anything stunning or remarkable about an individual learning some skills and then transmitting the skills to another; what is remarkable in this case is that simply by deciding to seize the opportunity to transmit their skills to others, these child abusers were able to transform the discrediting information about themselves into positive data, which subsequently enabled them to reject the stigma of child abuse and to alter their negative self-images. Few "rehabilitative" programs for child abusers at any level, whether part of the private or public sector, offer the opportunity to their participants to graduate from the stigma that defined their need of rehabilitation to begin with. The major flaw in these programs is their lack of an affiliation clause; i.e., the sequence of social experiences while involved in the program is not followed by an emergence of motivational awareness influenced by the individual's desire to create from those experiences a life's work.

Some contend that individuals pursue deviant and/or criminal careers chiefly because they identify with individuals who find that same behavior acceptable (Glaser, 1956: 440); or because they can rationalize their behavior (Cressey, 1953: 93); or because they construct definitions of the behavior which effectively neutralize the behavior (Glaser, 1956); or because they have the capacity to admit to themselves their criminal and/or deviant actions (Hartung, 1965: 52). An idea that few appear to be advancing is that the utilization of techniques of self-avoidance and self-protection are *learned* just as surely as the criminal and/or deviant behavior is learned.

Another factor all too often ignored in studies of deviant or nonideal conduct has to do with the individual's inability to replace the nonideal conduct with somewhat-ideal conduct. During the course of our research we observed child abusers learning skills in what we call behavior replacement. The nonideal abusive behavior was replaced by somewhat-ideal nonabusive behavior; this behavior was learned actively and passively, i.e., by doing it and by watching others doing it. This was followed by a desire to teach others behaving nonideally about behavior replacement and to equip them with the skills to accomplish it.

This process of change in reaction and self-definition is by no means a process unique to child abusers in self-help group therapy.

Barbara S. Heyl (1975) speaks of the identity transformations of prostitutes in house-training; Deborah W. Feinbloom (1975) discusses the same issue in articulating the problems of "passing" faced by transsexuals; Prudence Rains (1969) describes the process of becoming an unwed mother as one involving self-image redefinition.

Child abuser, prostitute, transsexual, and unwed mother all change in the process of *becoming*, and in that process experience "turning points" (Lofland and Stark, 1965: 870-1). These turning points increase their awareness and their desire to take some sort of action. They are situations in which old obligations diminish and lifestyles change, to be replaced by new involvements which become desirable and possible.

What we have found out by observing child abusers involved in self-help group therapy is how individuals can come to do what they initially view as unacceptable and in what terms they come to view their behavior as acceptable.

We also found that what Parents Anonymous offers its child abusers is really no different from what *Tally's Corner* offered its streetcorner men, and what the neighborhood tavern offers its patrons—a place of refuge from an impersonal world and of uncritical acceptance, a place which makes the prospects of tomorrow faceable. Like *Tally's Corner* and the neighborhood tavern, Parents Anonymous becomes for its members the beginning and the center of social life.

> What does Parents Anonymous do that helps a person with an abuse problem? Abuse is only a symptom of many other problems, often life-long problems. Parents Anonymous therapy can help...it provides the moral support it takes to keep going from day to day. Parents Anonymous is that someone to turn to when there is no one to care...that someone who will understand and offer help without condemning you to hell for what you've done. Our weekly group meetings are a source of practical, concrete suggestions that tell us just what we have to do to be able to cope with our children, our problems, and with ourselves. We are not struggling with abuse so much as we are struggling with ourselves...it offers unqualified friendship. This is something that most abusers have never in their life known. Attending a weekly meeting and just getting away from our every-day stressful situation helps us to step back out of the problem for a minute to see what's really going on. Our weekly meetings and telephone contact with other members has been priceless to me in learning to deal with the problem effectively and overcome it. Parents Anonymous has brought about two big "firsts" in my life. For the first time in my life I

like myself. For the first time in my life I have a friend. I still need every bit of the support Parents Anonymous gives me, but I no longer *feel* like an abusive person, because thanks to Parents Anonymous, I'm *not* an abusive person any more. We don't want to hurt our children. We don't know how *not* to hurt them. Constantly humiliating a child can hurt a lot more than a broken bone. And broken bones heal—emotional wounds often don't heal. I yelled at my baby a lot. He was a burden to me and I made sure he knew it. I didn't pick him up unless I had to, and then, not very lovingly, to say the least. I force-fed him when he didn't want to eat, and then got angry when he spit up the food. I called him ugly names in a hateful tone of voice. I was always angry about something and assumed that the baby was the cause of my anger. If I didn't have the damn baby I wouldn't have a problem. I blamed my constant screaming and anger on my husband and our poor financial situation. Every time I had a fight with my husband I screamed at the baby a little louder and longer. I felt constantly harrassed by this child. He thought his name was "shut up" because that was my usual greeting to him. These are the things that prompted me to join Parents Anonymous. I was afraid—afraid of my violently intense feelings and afraid of myself; afraid of the depression that was deepening day by day. Do these sound like the crimes of a despicable child killer? These kinds of things occur between most parents and their children. Unfortunately, most parents don't realize the damage they are doing to themselves and their children. Always reacting to a child in a negative way is abusive to the child and self-abusive to the parent. Am I really so different from any of you? Are any of you really so different from any of us in Parents Anonymous?

(Written by a Parents Anonymous member who participated in the study, April 1974)

Question: In recalling your childhood, do you think you were abused as a child?

Response: Uh huh.

Question: How? In what why?

Response: Sexually....

Question: Were you molested?

Response: Yeah, by my father, my *real* father...

Question: How old were you?

Response: Seven and thirteen...it happened twice both

times...and then beatings, too. My father used to hit me with his fists, break broom handles over our heads, kick us, throw us around, never broke our bones...we were lucky, we had a lot of bruises on us though. He'd keep us home from school so he wouldn't get in trouble 'til our bruises healed up.

Question: You remember all of that?

Response: Yeah.

Question: In remembering all of that, does it have any importance for you as a Parents Anonymous member? Those memories, do they play any kind of a role?

Response: As far as my kids are concerned?...Yeah, but I...I'm not...in a way I am a lot like my father as far as I'll hit on my kids, and you know kids are going to cry if you hit them, and in that way I'm like him because I'll hit them, and I can't stand for them to cry. I'll just say, "Shut up, *now*, or I'll hit you again, you know, so shut up!" That's what my dad used to do to me, and I don't know...I guess I'm just the way they taught me to be...I do my kids the same way, you know...not exactly the same way, because I don't do everything to my kids that my daddy did to me.

Question: Do you think in going to Parents Anonymous it will help you change some of those ways?

Response: Yeah, I wouldn't want my kids to grow up and be like me, you know, and then they'd treat their kids the same way....I want my kids to be different. I want to be able to love my kids, and I hope that one day I'll be able to, really, because I know how important it is. I've looked high and low for a father I've never really had ever since I can remember....I've always wanted somebody to just take me in their arms and just hold me, just hold me for what I am, you know, not for my sex or my body...and I'm still that way a lot...I'm still looking....I think the world of my doctor and my psychiatrist and I look up to him as my father, really, the only father I've had, and I think that if I had to choose between him and my father, I'd choose him, I'd just let my father go, you know. My father would do anything for me as far as money or food, but as far as baby-sitting for my kids, forget it! But in a really tight situation, I just go to P.A....(Interview #30)

INTERVIEW SCHEDULE

A. Natural history from feeling like a child abuser to affiliating with Parents Anonymous

1. Could you tell me where you were and what you were doing when you first suspected that you were a child abuser or that you had a problem with child abuse?

   Probe: What did you do?

   Why? How?

   Whom did you talk to?

   What about?

   Why them and not others?

   What was their response?

   How did their response affect you? Were you pleased, surprised, frustrated, comforted, etc.?

   What was their suggestion(s)?

   Had you considered any alternatives?

   If yes, what?

   Probe: suicide

   homicide

   foster-care for the child(ren)

   adoption

   abandonment

   marriage

   divorce

   abortion

   prostitution

   working

   counseling

   self-commitment (institutionalization)

   drugs

2. Before you became a parent, what did you expect it would be like? What did you think it was going to be like to have a child?

B. Affiliating with Parents Anonymous

1. How did you first hear about Parents Anonymous?

What did you think about the organization?

2. What did you think other members would be like?

3. What did you think happened at the meetings?

4. What did you expect/want out of Parents Anonymous when you went for the first time?

5. Were you invited to join the first time? By that I mean, were you invited back to another meeting?

6. During the first time, was it communicated to you what was expected of you if you joined?

7. If yes, what was expected? Who told you?

8. How long have you been a member of Parents Anonymous?

9. That first time you went, did you feel apprehensive, hostile, or scared? Do you ever have those feelings now when you go to a meeting?

10. Do you feel apprehensive about new "first timers," people coming to a meeting for the first time? If yes, does the apprehension have anything to do with the fact that you might meet one of your neighbors or friends at a meeting? If not, then what makes you feel apprehensive?

11. Do you do or have you done anything to prevent people from finding out that you are a member of Parents Anonymous?

12. Are you or were you more careful with some people so they won't find out that you are a member of Parents Anonymous?
    Probe: People such as your
    mother
    employer
    spouse
    child(ren)
    child(ren's) pediatrician
    child(ren's) schoolteacher
    or day care center worker

13. Do you do anything in particular to draw attention to the fact that you are a member of Parents Anonymous?

> Do you do any fund raising for the organization?
>
> Do you wear any buttons, display stickers, or banners of the organization?
>
> Do you help distribute any of the organization's Parents Anonymous literature?
>
> Are you involved in speaking to local groups about Parents Anonymous?
>
> Do you do any kind of publicity work for the organization?
>
> If yes, what kind?

14. In relation to any of the above questions, have you ever had any awkward experiences? If yes, please describe.

15. Were you ever "caught" by someone when you were unprepared to explain your activities and interest in Parents Anonymous? By that I mean, has anyone ever found out that you are a member of Parents Anonymous when you weren't prepared for them to find out?

16. If yes to #15, please describe the incident and who was involved. What were your feelings about the incident?

17. Does your Parents Anonymous group allow visitors to weekly meetings?
Probe: press people
social workers
nurses
policemen
doctors
teachers

Why or why not?

18. If yes, who is allowed to visit and how many times?

19. Why are some people "okay" as visitors and others not?

C. Child rearing experiences prior to and subsequent to affiliation with Parents Anonymous

20. Could you tell me how you used to feel about people who are child abusers?

21. Did you find yourself fitting into that description? If yes, please explain. If no, why not?

22. Do you feel that they are all the same with similar problems in life? Please explain.

23. What did being a child abuser mean for you?

24. Has your affiliation with Parents Anonymous affected your feelings about people who abuse their child(ren)? Please explain how.

25. Do you still identify with the former description of child abuser that you had? If yes, why? If no, why not and how did it change?

26. Do you still consider yourself a child abuser? If yes, why?

27. If no to #26, are you still a member of Parents Anonymous? Why?

28. Could you give me an idea of what you think the term child abuse means? Before you became involved with Parents Anonymous, did you have any idea what child abuse or being a child abuser meant?

29. Do you think that Parents Anonymous has affected your definition at all?

30. Please describe an incident or experience in which you considered yourself abusive to your child.

31. Refer back to #28: With regard to child abuse and child abusers, how did you get your information, from whom or what?
    Probe: newspapers
    television

radio
books (what kind)
family (nuclear or extended)
social worker/case worker
clergy
family doctor
emergency room nurse
policeman

What was the nature of the information you received?

32. Have you ever had occasion to use an emergency room of a hospital for injuries on your child(ren) that you had inflicted? If yes, explain.

33. Have you ever had occasion to use an emergency room of a hospital for injuries accidentally inflicted on your child(ren)? Please describe the incident.

34. How old were your children (or child) when you joined Parents Anonymous?

35. What were you like with the child(ren) before you joined Parents Anonymous? What were your feelings about the child(ren)?
Probe: hate
love
jealousy
distrust
resentment
pride
inadequacy
fear
guilt
Please explain.

36. Do you feel your affiliation with Parents Anonymous has changed you in any way? How? What has changed?

37. Have your feelings about your child(ren) changed? How?

D. Prior affiliation experiences and the Parents Anonymous experience

38. Have you ever been affiliated with any other group(s) before joining Parents Anonymous? If yes, what group(s)?

39. Did your involvement with that group have any kind of effect on you? If yes, what was the effect? If no, why not?

40. If yes to #38 and #39, were any problems created for you by your previous group affiliation? If yes, what were they? How did you handle them?

41. Have any problems been created for you by your experience as a Parents Anonymous member? If no, why not? Why the difference between your previous group and Parents Anonymous? If yes, please explain.

42. Have any problems been created for you as a Parents Anonymous member between you and your spouse, social worker/counselor, parent(s), child(ren). If yes, please explain.

43. Could you be specific and tell me how Parents Anonymous helps?

44. In reading some of the Parents Anonymous literature I have run across the word "alternative." Could you tell me what an alternative is?

45. Do you use alternatives? If no, why not? If yes, could you give me a specific example or an incident where you use(d) alternatives?

46. Where or from whom did you first hear about alternatives?

47. Do other members in your group use alternatives? How do you know?

48. Do you feel that you've changed in any way since you've started using alternatives? If yes, please explain how. If no, why not?

49. If you were to compare or contrast other groups that you've been a member of to Parents Anonymous, what would you say is unique or different about being a member of Parents Anonymous?

50. What do you usually talk about at your Parents Anonymous meetings?
    Probe: Child abuse (specifically or in general)
    getting a (better) job
    alternatives
    going to school
    spouses/boyfriends/girlfriends
    the "games people play"
    sex
    going to prison for your behaviors
    your childhood
    (In what context are the above discussed?)

51. Do you ever talk to or see other members of Parents Anonymous during the week? Are they social visits or part of the Parents Anonymous program?

52. If yes to #51, what do you talk about?

53. Is talking to other members during the week considered an alternative? If yes, how?

54. Have you ever been punished or reprimanded by the group? If yes, could you describe the experience or the incident?

55. Have you ever punished or reprimanded another member in the group? If yes, could you please describe the experience or incident?

56. Has your group ever had to kick anyone out of the group? If yes, could you please describe what led to the ousting and how it was carried out and by whom?

57. Would you say that not doing one's Parents Anonymous "homework" or not using alternatives can get someone kicked out of the group?

58. Do you think that there is a time limit that a group or group leader will tolerate before the member is punished, reprimanded, or kicked out?

59. Would you say that the changes within you came about because you did or are doing your Parents Anonymous "homework" and/or because you are using alternatives? If yes, could you be specific?

60. Has your involvement with Parents Anonymous helped you in some specific ways?
    Probe: in getting a (better) job
           in preventing you from physically abusing your child(ren)
           in joining other groups
           in pulling out of other groups
           in handling yourself
           in handling your marriage/divorce/love-life

61. Do you feel that your image of yourself has changed since you've been a Parents Anonymous member? If yes, please explain how and what has changed.

62. In recalling your childhood, do you feel that you were abused as a child? Please explain.

63. Did or do your childhood recollections have any importance for you as a Parents Anonymous member?

E. Face Data

64. Occupation _____

65. Religion _____

66. Age _____Sex _____

67. Marital Status _____How long?_____

68. How many times married _____

69. Number of children _____Ages_____

70. Children's sex _____

71. Spouse's occupation _____

72. Spouse's age _____

73. Is spouse the mother of the children? _____

74. Is spouse the father of the children? _____

75. Are you the mother of the children? _____

76. Are you the father of the children? _____

77. Who is at present living in the home? _____

78. Years of formal schooling_____

INTERVIEW INFORMATION

INTERVIEW # _____

Member:_____
Chairperson: _____ Chapter
Subject: _____

Date of interview:

Length of Interview: hrs.

Starting time:_____
Completion time: _____

General assessment of interview setting:

General assessment of interviewee's manner during the interview and credibility of his or her responses:

INTERVIEW NOT TAPED _____
    OR
INTERVIEW TAPED WITH RESPONDENT'S
    PERMISSION _____

BIBLIOGRAPHY

Akers, Ronald L. *Deviant Behavior: A Social Learning Approach,* Parts 1, 2, and 5. Belmont, California: Wadsworth Publishing Co., Inc., 1973.

Bakan, David. *Slaughter of the Innocents: A Study of the Battered Child Phenomenon.* Boston: Beacon Press, 1971.

Banfield, Edward C. *The Unheavenly City.* Boston: Little, Brown & Company, 1970.

Beck, Bernard. Cooking welfare stew. In Habenstein, Robert, W. (ed.) *Pathways to Data.* Chicago: Aldine Publishing Company, 1970.

Becker, Howard S., Strauss, Anselm. Careers, personality, and adult socialization. *American Journal of Sociology* 62:253-263, 1956.

Becker, Howard S.; Geer, Blanche; Hughes, Everett C; Strauss, Anselm. *Boys in White.* Chicago: The University of Chicago Press, 1961.

Becker, Howard S. *Outsiders: Studies in the Sociology of Deviance.* New York: The Free Press, 1963.

Becker, Howard S. *Social Problems: A Modern Approach.* New York: John Wiley & Sons, Inc., 1966.

Becker, Howard S. Introduction to *The Jack Roller,* by Clifford R. Shaw. Chicago: University of Chicago Press, 1966.

Blalock, Hubert M., Jr. *Social Statistics.* New York: McGraw-Hill, 1972.

Burton, Gabrielle. *I'm Running Away from Home but I'm Not Allowed to Cross the Street.* New York: Avon Books, 1975.

Cressey, Donald. *Other People's Money.* Glencoe, Illinois: The Free Press, 1953.

Davidson, Leonard. Counter-cultural organizations and bureaucracy: Limits on the revolution. Presented at the American Sociological Association annual meetings. San Francisco, August 1975.

Davis, Fred. Comment on initial interaction of newcomers in Alcoholics Anonymous. *Social Problems* 8:364-365, 1961.

DeCourcy, Peter, and DeCourcy, Judith. *A Silent Tragedy: Child Abuse in the Community.* New York: Alfred Publishing Co., Inc., 1973.

de Mause, L. Our forbears made childhood a nightmare. *Psychology Today* 8:85-87, 1975.

Denzin, Norman K. *The Research Act: A Theoretical Introduction to Sociological Methods.* Chicago: Aldine Publishing Company, 1970.

Ebeling, Nancy B., and Hill, Deborah A. *Child Abuse: Intervention and Treatment.* Acton, Mass.: Publishing Sciences Group, Inc., 1975.

Eglash, Albert, Youth anonymous. *Federal Probation* 22:47-49, 1958.

Elmer, Elizabeth, *Children in Jeopardy: A Study of Abused Minors and Their Families.* Pittsburgh: University of Pittsburgh Press, 1967.

Erikson, E. *Childhood and Society.* New York: W.W. Norton & Company, Inc., 1950.

Feinbloom, Deborah H. Goffman in drag: Transsexuals, stigma management, and labelling theory. Presented at the American Sociological Association annual meetings. San Francisco. August 1975.

Galdston, Richard. Observations on children who have been physically abused and their parents. *American Journal of Psychiatry.* 122:440-443, 1965.

Garfield, Harold, *Studies in Ethnomethodology.* Englewood Cliffs, N.J.: Prentice-Hall, Inc., 1967.

Gelles, Richard J. Demythologizing child abuse. *The Family Coordinator.* 135-141, 1976.

Gil, David G. *Violence Against Children: Physical Child Abuse in the United States.* Cambridge, Mass.: Harvard University Press, 1970.

Giovannoni, J. M. Parental mistreatment: Perpetrators and victims. *Journal of Marriage and the Family* 33:649-657, 1971.

Glaser, Daniel. Criminality theories and behavioral images. *American Journal of Sociology* 61:433-444, 1956.

Goffman, Erving, *Asylums: Essays on the Social Situations of Mental Patients and Other Inmates.* Garden City, N.J.: Anchor Books, 1961.

Goffman, Erving, On cooling the mark out. In Rose, A. (ed.) *Human Behavior and Social Processes.* Boston: Houghton Mifflin

Company. 1962.

Goffman, Erving. *Stigma: Notes on the Management of Spoiled Identity.* Englewood Cliffs, N.J.: Prentice-Hall, Inc., 1963.

Habenstein, Robert W. *Pathways to Data.* Chicago: Aldine Publishing Company, 1970.

Hartung, Frank E. *Crime, Law, and Society.* Detroit: Wayne State University Press, 1965.

Helfer, Ray E., and Kempe, C. Henry. *The Battered Child.* Chicago: The University of Chicago Press, 1968.

Heyl, Barbara Sherman. *The House Prostitute: A Case Study.* Unpublished Ph.D. dissertation, University of Illinois at Urbana-Champaign, 1975.

Holmes, J. Steven and Cureton, Edward C. Group therapy interaction with and without the leader. *The Journal of Social Psychology* 81:127-128, 1970.

Hughes, Everett C. *The Sociological Eye: Selected Papers On Work, Self, and the Study of Society.* Chicago: Aldine-Atherton, 1971.

Kanter, R.M. *Commitment and Community.* Cambridge, Mass.: Harvard University Press, 1972.

Kay, Barbara A. *Differential Self-Perceptions Among Female Offenders.* PhD. thesis, Ohio State University, 1961.

Kemp, Tage. Physical and psychological causes of prostitution. Geneva League of Nations Advisory Committee on Social Questions, No. 26, May 28, 1943.

Kitsuse, John I., and Spector, Malcolm. Social problems and deviance: Some parallel issues. Presented at the American Sociological Association annual meetings. San Francisco. August 1975.

Kleiner, Robert J., and Zahn, Margaret A. Sociological roles in evaluating a rehabilitation program. Presented at the American Sociological Association annual meetings. San Francisco. August 1975.

Konopka, Gisela. *The Adolescent Girl in Conflict.* Englewood Cliffs, N.J.: Prentice-Hall, Inc., 1966.

LeMasters, E.E. *Blue-Collar Aristocrats.* Madison: University of Wisconsin Press, 1975.

Lemert, E. *Social Pathology,* New York: McGraw-Hill, 1951.

Liebow, Elliot. *Tally's Corner.* New York: Little, Brown &

Company, 1967.

Light, Donald, Jr. Goffman revisited: The nature of moral careers. Presented at the American Sociological Association annual meetings. San Francisco. August 1975.

Light, R.J. Abused and neglected children in America: A study of alternative policies. *Harvard Education Review* 43:556-598, 1974.

Lindesmith, Alfred R. *Opiate Addiction.* Bloomington, Ind.: Principia Press, 1947.

Lofland, John. *Analyzing Social Settings.* Belmont, Calif.: Wadsworth Publishing Co., Inc., 1971.

Lofland, John, and Stark, Rodney. Becoming a world-saver: A theory of conversion to a deviant perspective. *American Sociological Review* 30:862-875, 1965.

Lopata, Helena Z. *Occupation: Housewife.* New York: Oxford University Press, 1971.

Lundberg, George A., Shrag, Clarence C., and Larsen, Otto N. *Sociology.* New York: Harper & Bros., 1954.

Matza, David, *Becoming Deviant.* New York: Prentice-Hall, Inc., 1969.

McCall, George J., and Simmons, J.L. (eds.). *Issues in Participant Observation.* Reading, Mass.: Addison-Wesley Publishing Co., Inc., 1969.

McKinney, John C. *Constructive Typology and Social Theory.* New York: Appleton-Century-Crofts, 1966.

Mead, George Herbert. *Mind, Self, and Society.* Charles W. Morris (ed.). Chicago: The University of Chicago Press, 1940.

Merton, Robert K. *Social Theory and Social Structure.* London: The Free Press of Glencoe, 1957.

Miller, Delbert C. *Handbook of Research Design and Social Measurement, 2nd Ed.* New York: David McKay Co., 1971.

Mothers anonymous, *McCalls* 99:57 January, 1972.

Murphy, Patrick. *Our Kindly Parent, the State,* New York: The Viking Press, 1974.

Pavenstadt, Eleanor. A comparison of the child-rearing environment of upper-lower and very low lower-class families. *American Journal of Orthopsychiatry* 35:89-98, 1965.

Polansky, Norman A., Borgman, Robert D., and DeSaix,

Christine. *Roots of Futility,* New York: Jossey-Bass, Inc., 1972.

Pollak, Otto. *The Criminality of Women,* Philadelphia: The University of Philadelphia Press, 1950.

Rains, Prudence. Becoming an unwed mother. Ph.D. thesis, Northwestern University, Evanston, Ill., 1969.

Ryan, James. *Suffer the Little Ones.* Nashville, Tenn.: Aurora Press, 1972.

Sanders, William B. *The Sociologist as Detective: An Introduction to Research Methods.* New York: Praeger Publishers, Inc., 1974.

Schatzman, Leonard, and Strauss, Anselm L. *Field Research: Strategies for a Natural Sociology.* Englewood Cliffs, N.J.: Prentice-Hall, Inc., 1973.

Scott, Robert A. *The Making of Blind Men.* Hartford, Connecticut: Connecticut Printers; New York: Russell Sage Foundation, 1969.

Selltiz, Claire, Jahoda, Marie, Deutsch, Morton, and Cook, Stuart W. *Research Methods in Social Relations.* New York: Holt, Rinehart and Winston, 1959.

Solzhenitsyn, Aleksandr I. The Nobel Lecture on Literature, Thomas P. Whitney (trans.). New York: Harper & Row Publishers, 1972.

Spinnetta, J.J., and Rigler, D. The child abusing parent: A psychological review. *Psychological Bulletin* 77:296-304, 1972.

Steinmetz, Suzanne K., and Strauss, Murray A., (eds.). *Violence in the Family.* New York: Dodd, Mead & Company, 1974.

Sumner, W. *Folkways.* New York: Dover Publishers, Inc., 1959.

Sutherland, Edwin H. Differential association. In *The Sociology of Crime and Delinquency.* Wolfgang, Marvin, Savitz, Leonard, and Johnston, Norman, (eds.) 2nd Ed. New York: John Wiley & Sons, Inc., 1970.

Sykes, Gresham M., and Matza, David. Techniques of neutralization: A theory of delinquency. *American Sociological Review* 22:664-670, 1957.

Webb, Sidney, and Webb, Beatrice. *Methods of Social Study.* New York: Longmans Green, 1932.

Webb, Eugene, Campbell, Donald T., Schwartz, Richard D., and Sechrest, Lee. *Unobtrusive Measures and Non-Reactive Measures in the Social Sciences.* Chicago: Rand-McNally & Company, 1966.

128

Zelditch, Morris, Jr. Some methodological problems of field studies. Edited by George J. McCall and J.L. Simmons. In *Issues in Participant Observation*. Reading, Mass.: Addison-Wesley Publishing Co., Inc., 1969.